Skills *in*
SOLUTION
FOCUSED BRIEF
Counselling & Psychotherapy

Series Editor
Francesca Inskipp

Skills in Counselling & Psychotherapy is a series of practical guides for trainees and practitioners. Each book takes one of the main approaches to therapeutic work and describes the core skills and techniques used within that approach.

Topics covered include

- how to establish and develop the therapeutic relationship
- how to help the client change
- how to assess the suitability of the approach for the client.

This is the first series of books to look at skills specific to the different theoretical approaches, making it ideal for use on a range of courses which prepare the trainees to work directly with clients.

Books in the series:

Skills in Transactional Analysis Counselling & Psychotherapy
Christine Lister-Ford

Skills in Person-Centred Counselling & Psychotherapy
Janet Tolan

Skills in Cognitive-Behavioural Counselling & Psychotherapy
Frank Wills

Skills in Rational Emotive Behaviour Counselling & Psychotherapy
Windy Dryden

Skills in Psychodynamic Counselling & Psychotherapy
Susan Howard

Skills in Gestalt Counselling & Psychotherapy, Second Edition
Phil Joyce & Charlotte Sills

Skills in Existential Counselling & Psychotherapy
Emmy van Deurzen & Martin Adams

Skills *in*
SOLUTION
FOCUSED BRIEF
Counselling & Psychotherapy

Paul Hanton

Los Angeles | London | New Delhi
Singapore | Washington DC

First published 2011

SAGE Publications Ltd
1 Oliver's Yard
55 City Road
London EC1Y 1SP

SAGE Publications Inc.
2455 Teller Road
Thousand Oaks, California 91320

SAGE Publications India Pvt Ltd
B 1/I 1 Mohan Cooperative Industrial Area
Mathura Road
New Delhi 110 044

SAGE Publications Asia-Pacific Pte Ltd
33 Pekin Street #02-01
Far East Square
Singapore 048763

Library of Congress Control Number: 2010938007

British Library Cataloguing in Publication data

A catalogue record for this book is available from the British Library

ISBN 978-1-84920-621-1
ISBN 978-1-84920-622-8 (pbk)

Typeset by C&M Digitals (P) Ltd, Chennai, India
Printed by MPG Books Group, Bodmin, Cornwall
Printed on paper from sustainable resources

CONTENTS

ABOUT THE AUTHOR

 Paul was born in East London in 1962. After a stint in the army at 18 years old, involvement with drugs and alcohol led to a four-year prison sentence at 22 for robbery; without any qualifications, there seemed to be no preferred futures, only escape from the problem present. However, while in prison Paul took five O levels; after prison, his A levels; and then surprised himself by completing a degree at Middlesex Polytechnic and finding that life had a bit more to offer.

Paul worked in student services and drug and alcohol services and got his first taste of SFBT, attending a two day course at The Brief Therapy Practice (BRIEF) in 1993. This course changed Paul's way of working with a client group that were often chaotic, transient and deemed 'difficult'. Paul took this way of working with him when he moved north to Barnsley to run one of the country's first dedicated young people's drug and alcohol projects.

In 2000, Paul enrolled on the world's first MA course in SFBT, run at Birmingham University by Bill O'Connell, with 14 other innovative and enthusiastic practitioners. He completed his MA in 2005, having undertaken his research into using SFBT with people living with moderate-to-severe depression attending a psychology department; he worked as a locum in that department until 2009. Paul has recently returned to young people's drug and alcohol work.

Paul is an accredited member of the British Association for Counselling and Psychotherapy (BACP) and in 2003, along with nine others, became a founding member of the United Kingdom Association for Solution Focused Practice (UKASFP).

PUBLICATIONS

Outrageous moments in therapy. In T. S. Nelson (Ed.), *Doing something different: solution-focused brief therapy practice*. Routledge, New York. 2010.

Solution-focused therapy in a problem-focused world. *Healthcare Counselling and Psychotherapy Journal*, 9(2). 2009.

Solution focused brief therapy with clients diagnosed as being moderately to severely depressed. *Research Review of the United Kingdom Association for Solution Focused Practice*, 1(1). 2008.

Solution focused therapy with carers. *Solution News*, 3(2). 2008.

The essential drug service commissioner, Drugscope, London. 2006.

An exploration of the effectiveness of using solution focused brief therapy with clients diagnosed as being moderately to severely depressed, MA. Dissertation, University of Birmingham. 2005.

The theory of not having theory in SFT. *Solution News*, 1(2). 2005.

Young people's substance misuse review: assessment of future needs, for Doncaster Drug Strategy Unit. 2005.

Solution focused therapy and substance misuse. In W. J. O'Connell, & S. Palmer (Eds.), *Handbook of solution-focused therapy*. London: Sage. 2003.

'Treatment toolkit': a review of publications related to treatment for substance misuse. Drug Prevention Advisory Service. 2001.

ACKNOWLEDGEMENTS

I am grateful to BRIEF for setting me on the Solution Focused path when I attended my first short course at what was The Brief Therapy Practice back in 1993 (or it may have been 1994).

I am indebted to Bill O'Connell, who believed in me enough to give me a place on the first MA in Solution Focused Brief Therapy in 2000, and in fact, to all the participants on that course who really gave me the freedom and confidence to start practising SFBT in more innovative and 'me' ways. Bill has always been a voice of balance and reason, one of the least dogmatic and client-centred therapists that I have met.

My wife Sue, my eldest son Christoph and my youngest son Kiyoshi have been inspirational in so many ways, not least reminding me that the world in which I work is just that, work; there is a life outside the workplace and the therapy room, something I believe in for the people I work with, but sometimes forget myself.

Last but not least, I'd like to acknowledge all the people who practise SFBT and Solution Focused Approaches in innovative and creative ways who have inspired me. There really are too many to list here and I do not want to 'miss' anyone out. I will have commented or thanked you outside this book and will probably do so again. This book is written by me, but owned by everyone who has contributed over the years in their own ways to my knowledge and learning.

PRAISE FOR THE BOOK

'Paul brings to the world of counselling and psychotherapy a fresh exposition of the solution-focused approach. Rich descriptions of the key solution-focused skills, illustrated with examples from Paul's extensive experience of practice, offer the reader many opportunities to extend their own practice repertoire. Drawing on his substantial training experience Paul brings the reader into a learning space, inviting you to engage with his ideas, reflect on how you might become more solution-focused in your work, and highlighting where to go next for further reading.'
John Wheeler MA, UKCP Registered Systemic Psychotherapist, independent solution-focused practitioner, trainer and supervisor (www.johnwheeler.co.uk)

'Paul is an experienced, skilled and innovative practitioner who has worked with a wide range of clients, some of them particularly challenging. This book introduces readers in a practical and accessible way to the nuts and bolts of how to practice in a Solution Focused way. I recommend it to newcomers to the approach and to others who wish to renew their practice.'
Bill O'Connell, Director of Focus on Solutions

'Written by one of the leading practitioners of solution-focused psychotherapy in the UK; this is a highly personal, and highly accessible introduction to contemporary skills in solution focused practice. It clearly states what it is about (and equally, what it's not about), and takes the reader, in true solution-focused style, on a series of small steps towards a clearly described, and well defined, conclusion. It makes use of clear outcomes and recaps in each chapter, clearly signposting for the reader the skills being discussed, and the relevance of them to practice. I was engaged, from the first page, by the level of detail with which this book is written, and the generosity of experience shared by the author. I would recommend this book to anyone wishing to explore, or re-explore, the skills of solution focused brief counselling and psychotherapy.'
Steve Smith, Lecturer in Mental Health, The Robert Gordon University, Aberdeen

1

INTRODUCTION

LEARNING OUTCOMES

By the end of this chapter the reader will:

- Understand the initial development of the Solution Focused Approach
- Understand 'where' SFBT is now
- Recognize the importance of this book as a skills book
- Understand the best ways to use this book

Skill: Noun. The ability to do something well.
(*The Oxford Dictionary of English*, 2006, Oxford University Press)

This book is a skills-based book. Skills are not to be confused with interventions and/or techniques, of which you will see many in this book. In truth, one cannot use an intervention or technique well without having the skills to use it, the skills to know when (and when not) to use it and the right 'ear' to know how what you are doing is being helpful.

This chapter will be the shortest chapter of the book. It is an introduction only. The real heart of the book lies in the skills-based chapters that follow. However, you will see that three terms in particular are used throughout this book, so I would like to begin with some key definitions. The main terms are:

1 SFBT
2 SFT
3 SFA

1 SFBT: SOLUTION FOCUSED BRIEF THERAPY

This is the proper term for the therapy described in this book and was the original name given to this unique therapy. The name is 'descriptive', reflecting the significance of language to the approach.

1a Solution

There is an understanding when using SFBT that the client is moving towards something they want to have happen, rather than moving away from something they do not want to have happen. This will be examined later in the book when looking at 'preferred futures'. In fact, a 'solution' does not always have a direct relevance to the presenting 'problem'. Again, more on this later.

1b Focused

There needs to be a focus on the work, a focus on the goals or preferred future outside the therapy room, so that the therapist and client are clear about why they are both there. There should be little meandering and sightseeing away from the job in hand. This is a unique factor in determining whether SFBT is actually being used as a therapeutic model or whether it is just some SF techniques that are being used.

1c Brief

This is often left out of the title these days and SFBT is often shortened to SFT (see below). The 'Brief' part of SFBT is to highlight that the work is focused and not open ended. However, 'brief' does not mean that we short-change our clients. People get what they 'need', not more. But we do not assume before we start therapy that clients will be 'in therapy' for years. My 'average' number of meetings with clients is five or six. The shortest number of meetings, of course, is one, and I have worked with one client for 31 sessions. Brief does not always mean quick.

It is important to note at this point that SFBT is not alone in the therapeutic world in being brief; there are many other therapeutic models that employ a 'brief' or time-limited version of their particular model of therapy. SFBT differs slightly by being brief in its original application.

1d Therapy

This is perhaps the most interesting part of the title as solution focused approaches and solution focused practice are used in many arenas with many different applications that are not therapy. Many of the original founders of SFBT were not in fact therapists, and some even insisted that what they did was not therapy. However, the 'therapy' part of SFBT is quite distinct, and yet, at the same time, very similar to other SF applications. The main differences from non-therapy applications of solution focus are in the setting, the 'contract', the expectations of the practitioner, in this case, the therapist, and the expectations of the client or 'customer'.

It is certainly acceptable to use solution focused principles, interventions and applications in non-therapy settings. However, it is the therapeutic application that this book addresses, and the skills required in this particular application.

2 SFT: SOLUTION FOCUSED THERAPY

Quite simply, all of the above, except the 'Brief' part of the title, has been dropped. This is a preference for many SF brief therapists nowadays as the term 'brief' seemed to convey a lack of seriousness of the approach and tended to imply that one could only use X number of sessions. In effect, the terms are interchangeable, and for the purpose of a skills-based book are not explored in great detail. I tend to use SFBT more than SFT, although I have no real preference. Interestingly, as SFBT has begun to drop the 'brief' part from the title, I have noticed a rise in other therapeutic approaches using 'brief' in their descriptions, such as Brief Psychodynamic Therapy, and there seem to be many more training courses in 'brief' applications of established therapeutic approaches. There is a slight difference in that 'time-limited' is different from brief, and SFBT is not a shortened, time-limited or pared down part of a wider model; it has been, and always will be, designed and developed to be brief in its entirety.

It is useful to know that there are a number of factors that have conspired to make brief therapies more attractive in recent times: there are economic issues in that individuals and companies do not want to pay for open-ended therapy (certainly insurance companies often will limit the amount of therapy they will pay for); practitioners want to be more focused in the work they do or, even better, clients are more mature in expressing their focused needs; and it may be that people are starting to take note of research suggesting that effective change can take place in fewer sessions over shorter timeframes.

3 SFA: SOLUTION FOCUSED APPROACHES OR SOLUTION FOCUSED PRACTICE (SFP)

It is true to say that since SFBT was first developed, practitioners from many disciplines around the world have found innovative ways to use and develop solution focused ideas and techniques. This can be seen in social work, nursing, coaching, team development, childcare, teaching, music and in many other areas of work. This book is not going to delve into these areas. Suffice to say, they are not counselling or psychotherapy, valid as they are.

The terms SFA and SFP have been growing as ways of describing instances where SF methods have moved away from the therapy room and the useful techniques, language and interventions founded in the therapy room are being used to great effect elsewhere. This is incredibly significant and probably truer for SFBT than for any other therapeutic approach. SF outside of therapy is probably bigger now than it is in therapy, It is also testament to the usefulness and versatility of the SF way of thinking. You will see SFA/SFP being utilized, for example, in the areas mentioned above and in:

- Mediation
- Coaching
- Anti-bullying work
- Occupational therapy
- Sports and activity settings
- Weight management programmes

There are many other areas too where the principles of SFBT have crossed over and are working well.

SFBT — IS IT?

You may also see in other books, training flyers and articles some of the following acronyms and terms (or different combinations of them): BSFT (Brief Solution Focused Therapy), CBFT (Cognitive Behavioural Focused Therapy), SOT (Solution Oriented Therapy). Although these approaches may well be valid and useful in their own right, they are not Solution Focused Brief Therapy and would not be recognized (by you) as such once you have read this book.

SOME MORE ABOUT THIS BOOK

The publishers have been very clear on this book being theory- and history-light. They have also been clear that the user of this book should be able to pick it up and use it in their training and/or practice without being bogged down in references and diversions to philosophical underpinnings and the like. Finally, the publishers have been clear that accessible language is used throughout. All of this is congruent with the solution focused approach, which aims to be accessible to people both practising and receiving therapy.

Such a brief, while being music to my ears initially, has not been entirely straightforward, though, because one cannot begin to use SFBT in the therapy room without at least a basic understanding of where it came from, why and how clients might benefit from it, and the major differences between it and the many other therapeutic approaches that are utilized today.

In the introductory chapter of *More Than Miracles* (2007: 1), in fact on the very first page, de Shazer et al. state that 'SFBT is not theory based, but was pragmatically developed'. The very nature of a pragmatic approach is that one can develop or refine it, and even diverge from it, as needed, and the concluding part of this chapter will touch upon this.

We, as solution focused brief therapists, do not retreat into a theory-laden, jargonized world that is a mystery to all but those who are 'experts' in the approach. We prefer to keep it simple, although as many SF practitioners will tell you, it is not easy keeping it simple and it takes a lot of practice to not allow yourself to fall into 'complicating' matters.

While the founders, proponents and practitioners of SFBT often talk of not having a theory, to the therapist or practitioner new to the approach, this 'atheoretical' aspect of the approach is often a dichotomy in that it can present itself as theoretical. De Shazer seems to be aware of this when he maintains that SFBT is 'without an underlying (grand) theory' (de Shazer et al., 2007). I think this means that we cannot ignore all theoretical thinking when talking about SFBT, especially as there are clear theoretical roots to the language and conversation that run through the spine of SFBT, but we should not let any theoretical thinking cloud our judgement and adversely affect the 'doing' of therapy and being with the client.

The following paragraphs will give the reader a brief outline of the pragmatic and evolving nature of SFBT. However, if you want to delve deeper, you will find some suggested book titles at the end of this, and every, chapter. My best hope for this book is that it manages to tread that line between being accessible to all and being thorough enough to satisfy those that want more than the basics. I also hope to pay due reference to the founders and developers of SFBT, while acknowledging that the 'new kids on the block' are equally important to the continuing development of SFBT.

WHERE DID SFBT COME FROM?

The solution focused approach to therapy was first described by de Shazer (1985) and de Shazer et al. (1986), having been developed at the Brief Family Therapy Center (BFTC) in Milwaukee. De Shazer et al. were heavily influenced by the work being undertaken at the Mental Research Institute in Palo Alto, California, and by family therapy (O'Connell, 1998). The primary developers, Steve de Shazer and Insoo Kim Berg, were also influenced by the work of Milton H. Erickson, an eminent hypnotherapist who de Shazer spent much time studying. Erickson believed in the uniqueness of each individual and their unique skills and ways of coping – this became a bedrock of SFBT.

The Brief Family Therapy Center was, as the name suggests, primarily working with families. The practitioners there developed some ideas that were based mainly on observations about what clients were telling them through their therapeutic sessions. It would seem that all the practitioners were extremely interested, from the outset, in finding out what was working for their clients and in doing more of it, an underpinning principle that has remained a key part of SFBT. As a family therapy centre, systemic family therapy was also influential, not least in that the practitioners saw their clients as part of a system that could not be ignored.

The ideas that the team were formulating were about how people coped despite what was going on in their lives. These ideas were about how people tended to concentrate on talking about and focusing on the problem areas while almost paying no heed to the exceptions (when the problem was less significant, or not there at all) even though the team noticed these more and more. The team developed their ideas into what was and wasn't needed in therapy in terms of interventions, techniques, focus and time. It is useful to note that while many of the team at the BFTC were therapists in their own right, two of the most influential people in developing SFBT, Steve de Shazer and Insoo Kim Berg, were in fact social workers. This meant that to some degree they were not confined to 'traditional' practice when it came to therapy. They took influences from many areas outside the therapy world and experimented with them in the therapy room.

Of course, this brief description cannot do justice to the origins of the approach or the hard work and thinking of the practitioners at the BFTC who developed and refined the approach, which has become a phenomenon in both the therapeutic and non-therapeutic world. Instead I would refer the reader to the many books that do explain the beginnings and original thinking behind SFBT more eloquently than I can (see the list at the end of this chapter).

As well as the skills, interventions and techniques that will be described in some detail throughout this book, practitioners of SFBT would recognize the following 'key beliefs':

1 Maintaining a future focus
2 Reframing problems and problem talk
3 Amplifying positive change and exceptions
4 Finding client-led solutions, based on the client's strengths, skills and resources
5 Believing that the client is the expert on their life.

These key 'beliefs' (as well as many other aspects of SFBT) represent a paradigm shift (de Shazer et al., 2007) from most of the traditional, and indeed modern, approaches to therapy which concentrate on the problem: understanding the problem, analysing and interpreting the problem, getting to the 'root' of the problem, managing the problem, moving away from the problem, and other focuses which are none the less still related to 'the problem'. SFBT concentrates on what is/has been/will be happening (differently) and looks beyond the problem. This paradigm shift is probably best summed up by O'Connell (2007: 385) when he states that SFBT 'does not believe that understanding pathology is necessary for the client to collaborate in search of solutions'.

Many well-trained psychotherapists, psychologists and psychiatrists may feel an initial discomfort in not attempting to understand the pathology of the problem(s). They may feel, based on their training, that they may 'miss' something. They may even feel that it is unethical to ignore or not explore signs and symptoms of more deeply-rooted issues that they should be treating. While I am sympathetic to such concerns, based on previous constructs, training and experiences, I am also reminded of the George Bernard Shaw quote: 'All evolution in thought and conduct must at first appear as heresy and misconduct'. Most new ideas in the therapy world, as well as in science, arts and literature, are difficult to grasp and appreciate initially. One of the nicest and most poignant things a client has ever said to me is that he had put our appointments on his wall calendar as seeing the 'not doctor'. He understood the 'paradigm shift'.

THE EVOLVING NATURE OF SFBT

After around a quarter of a century, one would expect to see an established therapy evolve, diverge and differ from the initial description of the model. This would be no different from any other therapeutic model. De Shazer and many of the founders of SFBT were clear that the 'model' was evolving and were pleased to see this evolution, as long as it stuck to the main principles of being solution focused. This statement itself represents a challenge to many SF brief therapists and SF practitioners. I have been on an international Solution Focused message list for over ten years and involved in the United Kingdom Association for Solution Focused Practice for over six years. In that time I have seen many attempts to define the essence of the main principles of SF and I've never seen total consensus, although there is of course a majority consensus on many tenets and beliefs (I discuss these in the next chapter). So what we sometimes see as SFBT now is a little different from what was initially described as SFBT. However, a good guide (apart from this book) as to whether SFBT is being adhered to is the EBTA (European Brief Therapy Association) research protocol, which can be found at: www.ebta.nu/page2/page30/page30.html. Remember though, a guide, which is what the EBTA protocol is, is only that, a guide. To be formulaic and restricted by any definition will take the solution focused brief therapist away from one of the main beliefs of the approach, which is to be client-directed in our work and not therapist-led.

THERE SEEMS TO BE THREE MAIN EVOLVING AREAS OF SFBT

When I say 'seems to be', I have to accept for myself, and make clear to the reader, that this is a personal reflection. Not every SF brief therapist would agree with my observations and assertions.

First, BRIEF (formerly The Brief Therapy Practice), which is the leader of solution focused training in Europe, has focused on the parsimonious nature of de Shazer's influence and has actively peeled away those parts of SFBT that it determines, through its client work, 'experiments' and team discussions, to be 'unnecessary' to the utilization of the model. BRIEF could be described as having a 'minimalist' approach to SFBT. In fact, some of what this organization does, as effective as it is (and it backs this up with its in-house client research), would not be seen as using all the established therapeutic 'steps' recognized by therapist accrediting organizations in many parts of the world.

BRIEF has to be respected for challenging the status quo in the therapeutic world, and there is no doubt that many practitioners (including those from other therapeutic approaches) would benefit from attending BRIEF training and learning of its approach. That said, it is but one approach to SFBT, and one area of the evolving nature of the model. BRIEF is not alone in this parsimonious approach and many SF brief therapists take this tack. Still, it is fair to say that BRIEF's methods are 'true' to de Shazer's continual reference to and use of Occam's razor, where the simplest of competing theories should be preferred. By this I mean that BRIEF continues to ask the minimum number of questions that enable change. This 'reductionist' approach is also based on a level of understanding and experience that equals that of the early work at the Brief Family Therapy Center in Milwaukee, where even the trainees (under de Shazer et al.) had Master's degrees and two years of clinical experience (Lipchik, 2002). The practitioners at BRIEF are equally experienced and qualified, and their experiments with minimalizing the approach are not simply borne out of thin air or a desire to be minimalist for minimalism's sake. It is this experience that drives the development of experimentation. Here is the fine line to tread – that of being driven by practitioner experience and still adhering to the principles of curiosity of client direction and being led by the client.

One criticism often heard of SFBT is that it is simply a set of techniques without an understanding of process. This is flippant and not true, and I hope the reader will understand this by the end of this book. This leads me on to another evolving area.

A second 'evolution' of SFBT is to make it more 'grounded' in the therapeutic processes, even in theory. Eve Lipchik, one of the original Milwaukee founders of SFBT (along with de Shazer et al.), has been vastly influential in this arena since the publication of her book *Beyond Technique in Solution-Focused Therapy* (Lipchik, 2002). While a quieter voice in the SF world than some, her book and approach have resonated with many therapists, myself included. We feel that there is more to SFBT and how it works successfully than simply applying techniques and/or questions. Equally, there are those in the SFBT world that disagree with Lipchik's divergence with some fervour. However, this book is not going to examine these differing views; it merely acknowledges them. I would not say that I wholly accept Lipchik's assertions, though her writings are worth reading. Other writers in the SF world, especially those who originally trained in other therapy approaches, tend to talk more about the therapeutic processes than did de Shazer and his followers.

Interestingly, to become an accredited psychotherapist in many national and international organizations there is a need to 'show' an understanding of how one's model (including SFBT) addresses many of the 'therapeutic' issues, for example forming an alliance, contracting and goal setting, closures, and so on. In my opinion, SFBT does address these matters well, and I will write of these matters in this book. However, there sometimes seems to be reluctance on the part of some SFBT proponents to acknowledge this. There can be, among some SF brief therapists, an aversion to even talking about theory, an almost 'anti-theory' of the approach which I sometimes wonder has simply become a *cause célèbre* among some practitioners.

The final evolving area of SFBT is where practitioners 'integrate' SFBT with other approaches. This can be done, for example: with Prochaska and DiClemente's cycle of change (Prochaska & DiClemente, 1983, 1986; see also O' Connell, 1998; Hanton, 2003). Some practitioners/therapists believe that as soon as integration happens SFBT ceases to be SFBT or that it is in some way 'watered down'. That may well be true, but this does not mean it is necessarily less effective. There is clearly a difference between practising SFBT as a 'whole' therapy approach (some use the word 'pure'; I don't) and using SF as a focus within another model or practice (this is SFA/SFP).

When teaching SFBT, or indeed SFA/SFP, to established practitioners and professionals in the therapy and non-therapy world, I take the SF understanding that I am not an expert in these practitioners' lives and practices. I accept that they may *begin* using SF by applying some of the interventions and techniques learnt in small, yet significant ways. They may then begin to use them more frequently until they eventually find a way of using SF as their main approach, which of course may not be therapy – it may be SFA/SFP. It is interesting that I have mentioned several well-known names in the SFBT world who started out as non-therapists. By integrating SFA/SFP in their professions, they then went on to become accredited therapists. I count myself among them.

Many of the readers of this book will begin by experimenting with or integrating SF interventions within their existing practice, as described above. They may then choose to develop their practice so that they use SFBT in its entirety with clients. It is my belief that either way is 'acceptable', though one could not say one is doing SFBT by simply applying some of the practice within a different approach.

My assertion would be to point to the inevitability of differences in therapeutic practice as the numbers of SF brief therapists grow, though also to make clear the difference between using Solution Focused Brief Therapy and using solution focused approaches. It is useful here to acknowledge this debate, without exploring it too far in a therapy skills-based book. The original founders of SFBT were open 'to whatever works' (Miller, 2008). This is sometimes forgotten by the partisan nature of some SF brief therapists.

FINALLY...

To write this book I have drawn on what is now over 16 years of SF practice, SF training and SF supervision, including nearly 3,000 hours of direct therapy. I have drawn on hundreds of conversations with skilled practitioners and therapists and very skilled clients. I have gathered exercises and 'snippets' from many places – my handouts, other people's ideas, and places I cannot even remember. If I do not thank people personally (usually because I can't remember the exact conversation or context), then I apologise. However, I will acknowledge from the start that while I have tried to put as much original thought into this book as I can, I am indebted to a great many people along the way.

Throughout the book you will see there are snippets of case studies, questions that have been asked and answers that have been received. They are all real or based on real client meetings. However, as one would expect, they have been heavily doctored so as to protect individuals' identities. As a caveat I would also point out that some of the examples given are not 'exact' words, but a recollection of conversations where I have not had notes to refer to.

You will meet Sally, a very interesting character and someone who presented a huge challenge to my normal pace and style. She is someone with whom I worked for a long time (for me). I struggled sometimes to maintain an SF focus with Sally, yet I trusted in the model.

You will also find some exercises: some personal ones and some to use with others, including clients. You will also find some photocopiable resources, pointers to further reading and links to some useful websites.

Enjoy this book. 'Dip in' to parts of the book as you need to — it is designed to do just that. Use the exercises, read further, visit websites and hopefully you and your clients will experience the liberation that SFBT brings to therapy sessions. My advice is to try to 'understand' the difference from the established therapy world that SF thinking brings without casting aside all that you know already.

As you read through the book please remember that while the techniques and interventions seem easy enough to use (as this book is designed to do), Solution Focused Brief Therapy 'takes time and experience to master, just like any other therapeutic approach' (Lipchik, 2002: 6).

RECAP: INTRODUCTION

This chapter has looked at the terms used throughout the book. It has also looked briefly at the origins of SFBT and how it has evolved 'til now, including in the non-therapy world (SFA/SFP). And it will have given the reader a clear idea that this is a skills-based book, and not theory- or jargon-heavy.

PERSONAL REFLECTION

Think about what you will use this book for, how you will know it has been a useful book, and how others might know that you are reading about or using SFBT and that it is in some way useful. Also think about how you will know that you are starting to understand what SFBT is, what are the clues that you 'get it'?

TRY THIS

Enter the terms 'Solution Focused Brief Therapy' and 'Brief Therapy' into a search engine on the internet and see how many 'hits' there are. Compare this with any other therapy approach and see the extent to which SFBT has become known, and for what.

KEY TERMS USED IN THIS CHAPTER

SFBT, SFT, SFA, SFP, Solution, Focus, Focused, Brief, Therapy, Approaches, roots, history, evolvement, de Shazer.

SUGGESTED FURTHER READING

George, E., Iveson, C., & Ratner, H. (1999). *Problem to solution* (2nd Edn.). London: BT Press.
BRIEF are hugely influential throughout the UK, Europe and beyond. This easy-to-read book is an excellent introduction to SFBT by three well-known BRIEF trainers.

Lipchik, E. (2002). *Beyond technique in solution-focused therapy*. New York: The Guilford Press.
Written by one of the original 'Milwaukee founders' of SFBT, we see in this book a marked departure from the parsimony associated with the model. Lipchik explores theory and emotions.

O'Connell, B., & Palmer, S. (2003). *Handbook of solution-focused therapy*. London: Sage.
A UK handbook, with chapters from many of the 'leading lights' in their respective SF fields, it covers group work, research, social work, and much more. Each easy-to-read chapter follows a similar format.

2

SFBT: SKILLS, ASSUMPTIONS AND WAYS OF WORKING

LEARNING OUTCOMES

By the end of this chapter the reader will:

- Appreciate the underlying assumptions of SF brief therapists about the people they see
- Understand the basic skills set needed to be a competent SF brief therapist
- Appreciate the differences in how an SF brief therapist works compared to other therapeutic ways of working

I have mentioned previously that de Shazer (and others) were influenced by the work of Milton H. Erickson. In a book about Erickson (Zeig & Munion, 1999) and his ways of working, a core assumption underlying Solution Focused Brief Therapy is outlined extremely well. It helps me to realize what de Shazer, Berg and the other founders were seeing in the development of SFBT as a coherent approach: 'The patient is the driving force in the treatment selection process – not the symptom, not a theory and not the therapist preferences' (Zeig & Munion, 1999: 89).

We see people as individuals with a unique set of beliefs, skills and resources to help them cope with their unique set of issues. These are some of the 'keys' that de Shazer talks about (de Shazer, 1985) and are undoubtedly connected to his readings and understandings of Erickson. SFBT utilizes these (client) skills and resources above our own as therapists so that the client can move forward. This is a fundamental belief: the client's resources move the client forward, not the therapist's knowledge, though there is a sharing of expertise that brings this to fruition.

We have seen how SFBT has continually evolved since its inception, and subsequently how some (almost) universally accepted assumptions, which underpin our work as therapists, have developed. I have split this chapter into parts so that the reader does not become confused by long lists:

- Assumptions and beliefs (part 1)
- Solution Focused skills (part 2)
- Questions we ask of ourselves (part 3).

PART 1: ASSUMPTIONS AND BELIEFS IN SOLUTION FOCUSED BRIEF THERAPY

SFBT does not espouse a theory so there is no definitive truth to be gleaned by a core set of 'commandments'. Rather, most solution focused brief therapists would agree that there are some core assumptions and beliefs that we agree on about the people we see and in the work to be done. Some of these assumptions and beliefs are briefly explained below. Most SF brief therapists that I have met, discussed and debated with would agree about these assumptions and beliefs.

1   The therapist is not the expert on the client and their context, the client is.
2   There may well have been some pre-session change.
3   Situations may appear static, but they are constantly changing.
4   There are always exceptions (to the problem) to be found.
5   The client does have skills, strengths and resources; they have used these before and can utilize them again.
6   The client is more than the presenting problem.
7   You do not 'need' to know all about the problem to build solutions.
8   Right and wrong, blame and fault, do not make things better.
9   A little change (for the better) is better than no change; no change is better than a deterioration or worsening situation.
10   Sometimes 'good enough' is good enough.
11   Everybody has a preferred future.
12   Language and meaning are socially constructed.
13   The time spent outside therapy is more important than the time spent with the therapist.
14   Recognizing what is right is more important than recognizing what is wrong.

1 The therapist is not the expert on the client and their context, the client is

However young or old the client is, they will always have more experience of themselves and their context than we will. This is a fact which cannot be overstated.

I find it personally and professionally almost offensive when I hear that an 'assessment has been done' on someone and this determines the work that needs to be done. This person may have lived 20 years (over 175,000 hours) or 30 years (over 262,000 hours) and we, as professionals, cannot possibly sum up in one hour all of that, and what is to be done.

> Patients have put faith in their [psychotherapists'] expertise and expect them to say what is wrong and how to put it right. Psychotherapists' understanding of patients' problems and knowledge about how they can be remedied is, however, very much less than they imagine. It is also less than the therapists imagine. (Mair, 1992: 135)

This is not to say that the therapist does not have a valuable contribution to make. We know about SFBT, we know about focusing conversations towards solutions, we know about co-constructing ways forward, we know about collaborative approaches, we know what may have been helpful for other people we have seen, we may even know about resources that might help. Above all, however, we know that the client knows about themselves: what has worked, what hasn't, what skills they have, what support networks they have, what they would like to happen and what they would like to stop happening.

We will share our expertise and learn from each other in order to be helpful for the client. It is this 'co-construction' of the therapy that departs somewhat from other therapeutic approaches, where clients tend to 'fit' therapist formulations and decisions on the outcomes of therapy that are then often determined by the therapist in keeping with the 'steps' in the particular model.

A solution focused brief therapist asks questions from a not knowing stance: not knowing about the client, not knowing about their problems, unique solutions, strengths, capabilities, support, what has worked previously, and exceptions to the problems. These are the things that a SF brief therapist is curious to know more about.

If we start from the expert position of knowing (or thinking we know) what will work with everyone we see, we cannot be client focused. It is our job to find out, to be curious and to listen. It is also our job to 'collaborate' with clients in finding solutions, not in telling them what they must do from a position of hierarchical expertise.

This collaborative stance is sometimes criticized from outside SFBT. It is mistaken as 'collusion' by therapists (and non-therapists) unfamiliar with the nuances of Solution Focused Brief Therapy. Giving space to the exploration of possible solutions requires considerable skills, as will become evident throughout this book. I heard a phrase at a recent conference: A client 'commissions our expertise'. In other words, they allow us to be experts when it is helpful for them. I like this phrase.

2 There may well have been some pre-session change

This will be looked at in greater detail in Chapter 4. All I will say here is that SF brief therapists believe that it is worth exploring anything that has happened recently – perhaps between the initial contact (referral) and the client seeing you for their first therapeutic meeting.

3 Situations may appear static, but they are constantly changing

The world is constantly changing. We change, our clients change, everything changes. Understanding this helps the SF brief therapist dislodge the experience of 'being stuck' that many clients refer to.

So if things are constantly changing, then sometimes they have got worse, and they can get better. They may have already been better at times or are currently 'getting' better. Things as enduring as depression, OCD (obsessive compulsive disorder), drug and alcohol problems, marital problems and schizophrenia all have minutes, hours, days or weeks when they are not affecting someone as much as at other times. The SF brief therapist explores these differences and changes, as small as they may be, for 'clues' that give the client and therapist insight into what has been helpful.

4 There are always exceptions (to the problem) to be found

Linked very much to point 3 above, if nothing is static, then there must be times when the 'problem' is not there or at least is not as prevalent. It is our role as therapists to look for those exceptions, to highlight them and to amplify them where possible. This focus on 'exceptions' will be addressed throughout this book.

5 The client does have skills, strengths and resources; they have used these before and can utilize them again

SF brief therapists do not believe that people come to us as dysfunctional, unskilful, helpless souls. Instead, they believe the opposite. SFBT places an emphasis on mental health (Berg & Miller, 1992) and what is working, rather than on the traditional, problem focused approaches that concentrate more on what is not working or what is 'wrong' with the person, which then requires treatment or intervention.

People come to see us at all ages and with many different experiences. They have their own unique support networks, their own unique coping strategies, unique strengths, unique skill sets and usually, once we probe a bit, unique and relevant stories to tell us that demonstrate these things. These things, once uncovered, become 'evidence' of competence, and this is confirmed by therapists highlighting these competencies and giving praise where it is appropriate.

When we view people as functioning, coping, managing individuals, we automatically have a different mindset in which we start the therapeutic process. We look for 'how' they are managing rather than 'why' they are not. This influences how and what we say to clients and doing this well is part of the skill of doing SFBT well.

This approach does not ignore or negate any difficulties. Far from it. We acknowledge and validate those difficulties and express genuine praise and wonder that the person sitting in front of us keeps going, somehow, with all that is going on.

6 The client is more than the presenting problem

A client who presents with depression, anxiety, OCD, substance misuse issues, self-esteem issues, and so on may also be a mother, a son, a husband, a friend, with all that this entails. There are most certainly times when their identity is not part of the problem, and the skill of the SF brief therapist is to actively highlight those exceptions. By doing so, we intentionally break down the problem construct with which people can identify themselves. They may have a job or have had a job. They may have hobbies. They will certainly have interests outside their presenting problem. By assuming that they are more than the presenting problem, we see things about them that we can help them realize and/or utilize in their movement towards their preferred future.

The presenting problem may be what they bring to us as therapists and what we need to acknowledge and validate, but to not recognize the 'whole' person is at the very least disrespectful and remiss; at the worse, it is neglecting our role.

7 You do not 'need' to know all about the problem to build solutions

This is perhaps the most misunderstood underpinning associated with SFBT. We are not saying here that we will not hear a problem or that the problem is seen as irrelevant. What we are saying is two things.

First, when someone wants to 'get rid' of a problem, traditional therapeutic methods often believe that the best way to do this is to explore, understand and come to terms with that problem, sometimes by 'picking' at it until it is dissected in small detail. 'Triggers', 'roots' and causes of the problem often become the focus of the therapeutic work. For the SF brief therapist, this is not as fruitful as finding out what the client wants to do instead of having the problem. Listening to the times when the problem was less or not there is deemed as more useful than constantly focusing on the problem. Listening to what the client does that is helpful is more important that listening to what they do that is unhelpful.

Secondly, the lack of exploration of 'the problem' is liberating for both the client and the therapist. Most models in the helping field seek to minimize, manage or get away from 'the problem'. This is why we hear people say 'When I had depression', 'When I was a junkie', 'Now I have beaten OCD', etc. This current identification of one with the past problem means, in my view, that people are inextricably linked with 'the problem'. By seeking a solution that is *instead* of the problem – 'I want to go to college', 'I want to be happy' – we allow, even encourage, people to view themselves as something else. Their identity becomes what they become, not what they were.

8 Right and wrong, blame and fault, do not make things better

When at home someone forgets to do a chore, giving them a hard time about it makes no one feel better. It may satisfy the chastiser in some small way, but it does not lead to good feelings for either party.

One of the things that I have heard in the therapy room time and time again is 'I was wrong to....', or 'I know XXX happened, it was my fault'. While this may be a self-identified move on the part of the client to acknowledge their part in 'the problem', it rarely moves people on into positive thoughts or actions, or when it does, it takes some time to do so. Likewise, and I would argue even more damaging, is if the therapist tries to get the client to acknowledge fault or blame.

Insoo Kim Berg, who contributed many skilful questions to SFBT, was particularly famous for the following phrase: 'You must have had a good reason for (doing) that'. This eloquent offering told her clients that she did not blame them or judge them for their actions, but rather accepted that their actions were determined to be their way of dealing with something at any given time.

Now clearly we are not going to applaud, condone or approve certain behaviours. In the same way we are not going to judge them. It is not our place to do so. Society, the courts, family and friends can all do either. It is our role to help people help themselves and in the SF brief therapist's view (although other therapies, such as person centred therapy, believe this too) blaming does not help people to help themselves.

A useful question to ask clients who constantly blame themselves for a set of behaviours or events is 'And what would you notice that tells you that you are dealing with this differently, maybe in a better way?' If someone is constantly blaming another person, we might utilize a questions such as 'Is it helpful for you to lay fault with them?' The emphasis on being helpful for 'you' is the important part. When I asked this question of someone who was blaming their mother for their worsening OCD by not putting ornaments in the 'right' place, they responded by saying 'Mmmm, I guess it is my choice whether I do my OCD things or not when that happens. I see what you mean'. I hadn't 'meant' anything; I was merely asking a question.

It is also useful to validate (as in other therapies) that some events are outside a client's control, so they could not have done anything about them even if they had wanted to. Again, as other therapeutic approaches would do, we should acknowledge that sometimes people act in certain ways as responses to certain triggers and should not be judged (including by themselves) for those responses.

9 A little change (for the better) is better than no change; no change is better than a deterioration or worsening situation

This takes little explaining. If someone is improving slightly this is good. We cannot always hope for leaps in improvement. In fact, small steps are, for many people, more realistic and sustainable and certainly better than not making any improvement at all.

Not changing at all may be seen by some therapeutic models as a lack of progress. Indeed, it may be seen by clients and therapists as frustrating when the purpose of coming to therapy, surely, is to get better. In SFBT we believe that no change indicates a couple of things. First, it indicates that someone is somehow coping with or managing their situation. This should be applauded and praised, and examined to give insight into what is helping this person manage or cope. I would always acknowledge this and explore it further with questions such as 'How are you managing this?' or 'What are you doing that is keeping you going?' Secondly, it shows that somehow the person has 'arrested' the decline – things have not become worse. How come? What are they doing that is stopping this decline? It is my job to find out.

These two factors are extremely important to SFBT. We assume that the person is not a passive bystander to their 'problem', that they are active in either coping with their lot or somehow stopping it from getting even worse. Such an assumption is evidence of competence at some level. This is a hugely important underpinning of the solution focused approach. We see people for their levels of functionability, not their dysfunctions; for their competencies, not their incompetence. Once we start to view people in this way it is amazing what can be uncovered and noticed by both therapist and client. This view of functionability, I have no doubt, helps the therapist to stay fresh in their approach and not to 'burn out'.

Whether a client starts to make changes slowly or not, there is an underlying assumption in SFBT that clients come to therapy wanting to change (O'Hanlon & Weiner-Davis, 1989), or why would they be there? We do not need to force the pace of that change, but simply recognize that change at some point is inevitable.

10 Sometimes 'good enough' is good enough

We will look later at 'scaling' and 'preferred futures' where people make clear what their best hopes are, what their ideal looks like. While we would never dismiss this as being impossible (with provisos such as waking the dead or walking when paraplegic, etc.), we need to accept, as does the client, that this may be some way off and may not be achieved in or outside therapy within specific timescales or given specific circumstances. We help people to understand that there are stages along their journey to their preferred future. These stages are important and sometimes there is a point which, while not the ideal, is 'good enough'.

A simple example of this might be a client who expressed in an initial meeting that their best hope would be 'to be successful, like other people'. For them, this entailed having a good job, being married, feeling confident and being happy. This was a 10 out of 10 life for this client. They came to the therapy room placing themselves at 2 out of 10 on the same scale. Some months later, when they were 6 out of 10 on their scale and had a confirmed place at university, they agreed that things were 'good enough' to stop coming to therapy despite not being married or feeling 'totally' confident or happy. They reasoned that now they had secured a university place, the other things would 'come along in time'.

11 Everybody has a preferred future

We believe that everyone who comes to see us wants something to be different, or else why are they there? Our job is to find out what it is they want, not what they don't want. A future related to the absence of a problem is a negative goal. Our task is to help them find what they would like to be doing 'instead'. The emphasis on the future in SFBT is of extreme importance. The past and present may be full of difficulties (although they may also contain examples of how those difficulties were/are being coped with and/or overcome), but it does not follow that the future has to contain the same difficulties. The future is not yet here.

It is important to note that a preferred future does not have to be inextricably tied to the problem. An example I often use in training is that the problem I have is that I hate practising my musical scales on the saxophone and I really wish that I could approach them with more joy and vigour. My preferred future, as uncovered by a trainee on a course I was facilitating (thank you), is to feel confident playing my saxophone on stage with other people. Now I still hate practising my scales, and, I have been on stage and felt confident. In the process, I realized that my problem was not related to scales practice, but was more to do with worrying about getting things wrong.

I make no apologies for including a personal example here. As with all therapies, if you believe it would work for you, then you will practise with more belief with your clients.

One well-known practitioner of SFBT, Yvonne Dolan, goes further than simply talking of a preferred future. In her book *Beyond Survival* (2000), she devotes a whole part of the book to 'Creating a Joyous Future'. This is nice.

12 Language and meaning are socially constructed

This assumption is a complicated one and there are books and writers that focus on social constructions, structuralism, poststructuralism and many other angles of philosophy and theory that have and do influence some of the SFBT thinkers. However, this is a skills-based book and as such it will not delve too far into theory or philosophy. In fact, it could be argued that a deep understanding of this is not needed to do therapy well.

And yet, to ignore the influence of social construction and other philosophy/theory on the developers and development of SFBT would be an omission too far.

There is no doubt that the 'thinkers' and philosophisers in the SF world have been hugely influenced by the correlation between what we do, what we understand and how we shape our experiences by the constructs of the world we live in, and especially by the language we and others use. I have touched on this by mentioning how people can be 'tied' to the problem of identity, how we are not experts on the client's context, and how our 'view' of the competent client influences how we speak to and hear clients. I will leave it there and encourage the reader, if they so wish, to read further. Wittgenstein, Foucault, Derrida, Bateson and some of de Shazer's writings will be helpful here. De Shazer was hugely influenced by the way words were/are used and explores this in both *Words Were Originally Magic* (1994) and in *More than Miracles* (de Shazer et al., 2007).

Not all SF brief therapists are as concerned with understanding such theories in depth as was de Shazer. You do not need to know of or understand the theories or theorists mentioned here to 'do' SFBT, though a skim of the literature at least is useful. SFBT is not simply a set of techniques, questions and words thrown together. There is a rationale behind what is said in the therapy room, what words are used and why.

13 The time spent outside therapy is more important than the time spent with the therapist

This is probably one of my 'favourite' assumptions, and one that keeps me grounded. When someone comes to see the solution focused (or indeed any) brief therapist, they may see us weekly, fortnightly, or at some other interval, for an hour, maybe slightly less, maybe slightly more. We may see them five times, or six, or maybe 15 times. Whatever the length and frequency of our meetings, it must be realized that this is a very small part of their lives, and that they spend much more of their time outside this contact than in it. The client may glean some insight in the therapy room (we hope), they may find their time spent with us helpful (we hope), but what they do 'out there' is what counts. We help them to use their time in therapy to help themselves away from therapy and when they do not need to come any more (the sooner the better) we should be pleased.

It is quite normal in the helping professions for the worker/therapist to receive a 'thank you' card from the client, but stop for a second and think about this. By accepting a card we are accepting that we are the instrument of change when actually the client is the instrument of their own change. If I get a card occasionally, I keep it, although I certainly never display it. What I have started to do recently when given a card is to read it, thank the client, and then put a message at the bottom, something like 'Thank you for letting me work with you. I couldn't have done it without you.' I then given the card back to the client. To display cards in your office/therapy room gives out a message that we are the instrument of change, when it is the client who is the instrument of change. We merely facilitate that change by asking the right questions and focusing the conversations. A client should leave us knowing that they can cope and thrive outside the therapy room. They should be empowered, not indebted. In addition, we should acknowledge, at the very least to ourselves, that we learn from each and every client.

14 Recognizing what is right is more important than recognizing what is wrong

If we explore what is 'working' for someone – the times when the problem is reduced or not there – and get them to do more of what is working, we automatically see a reduction in the problem without focusing specifically on it. Let me give you an example. Imagine a pie chart where a small segment, say 5%, is an illustration of what is working ('I feel a bit better when I manage to get out of the house'), and 95% of the pie chart represents all the things that are 'wrong' with that person's life. We can choose as therapist (and client) to work on that 95%, which seems like a big task, or we can choose to work on making the 5% maybe 6% or 7%, in which case the task does not seem so onerous, can be more focused and automatically leads to the 95% of what is wrong being reduced.

It is this focusing on and amplifying the positives that builds collaboration and encourages cooperation between client and therapist, and it owes much to the influence of Milton Erikson (Hayley, 1973). There is little doubt in my mind that working with someone on doing more things that are right for them, or noticing more when things are going well, is much more effective that the endless talking about what is going wrong and how bad it all is.

We do not, of course, ignore the bits that are not going well. We acknowledge and validate them, and we then look for opportunities to highlight the more positive aspects.

PART 2: SOLUTION FOCUSED SKILLS

Though I believe there is no set way to do SFBT, nor is there a theory written in tablets of stone, there are some basic beliefs and interventions, as outlined above. In this chapter I will also focus on some of the skills, as I do on training courses, so that the reader new to SFBT can 'grab the basics', and the reader who knows something of SFBT may organize their thoughts. This chapter only 'outlines'; the topics touched on here are discussed in more depth in subsequent chapters.

While I, and many others who practise SFBT, owe a huge debt to the founders and influencers of SFBT, I have, as I have already stated, deliberately not gone into the history of SFBT in depth as there are many good books out there that do this already (see further reading at the end of this chapter). I have sought to bring some originality to this text. I also intentionally want budding SF brief therapists to develop their own SF path, not ignoring the experts who came before, but also developing themselves.

Skills required by a solution focused worker

A solution focused worker will utilize the skills that many others in the caring professions utilize on a daily basis, such as listening and demonstrating warmth, acceptance, normalization and validation. These skills are what I call the 'common currency' of therapy and caring.

The additional skills used by the solution focused worker or, in this book, therapist, are by no means confined to or exclusive to solution focused work. Indeed, as it is the nature of the solution focused worker/therapist to help the client realize and utilize their own unique skills, so the solution focused trainer and/or author will help course participants and text readers realize and hone their existing skills, I often tell people: *A solution focused worker needs to 'hone' certain skills, not throw away the skills they already have.*

Clearly, some skills, grounded in a problem focused approach, are not generally used in SFBT and rather than 'force' people to abandon these skills immediately, it is the belief of many solution focused practitioners that by focusing on the development of solution focused skills, the problem focused skills will soon become redundant or at least less pervasive. This is a mirror of the way we work with clients, and as I will highlight later in the book, supervision and training in SFBT follow the same principles and assumptions and employ the same skills as the therapy itself.

The skills listed below are not to be confused with the techniques and interventions that they relate to. Rather, they are to be viewed as 'how to' use the techniques and interventions. It is the 'how to' that is the skill, not the intervention itself. In addition, all of the skills listed below are examined or explored in more detail throughout the book. So what are these skills that need to be honed?

The list below is, I hope, useful. However, there is one prerequisite that is not exclusive to SFBT (so is not listed) that comes up again and again. That is to **listen**. Listen for what the client wants, listen to what they say, so that you can ask the next question based on the last answer: this is the way a SF brief therapist would approach the therapeutic 'formulation'. Listen with a curious ear and do not presume to ask anything if it is not based on what you have heard. This has been described by some SF practitioners as 'relentless listening'. In fact, when I asked on an international message list what other practitioners would include in an essential skills book, listening came out way on top. This was followed by asking the right questions.

Here, then, are the skills required by a solution focused brief therapist:

1 The ability to engage in problem-free talk.
2 The ability to explore any pre-session change.
3 The ability to listen actively for client strengths, resources and skills, and any past or present utilization of those skills.

4　The ability to elicit from the client a preferred future and co-construct a rich image or narrative of that future.
5　The ability to look for exceptions and differences.
6　The ability to be able to take a non-expert stance towards the client's experiences and constructs.
7　The ability to utilize the 'miracle (wonderful) question'.
8　The ability to utilize scaling.
9　The ability to be sensitive to using 'and' and not 'but'.
10　The ability to be sensitive to using 'how' and not 'why'.
11　The ability to give genuine compliments and praise to a client.
12　The ability to negotiate a task outside therapy that is related to the client's movement towards a preferred future.

1 The ability to engage in problem-free talk

Problem-free talk is examined and illustrated in much more detail later in this book so I am not going to go into detail here. Suffice to say, I believe that problem-free talk is about simply talking and listening. It is not about 'doing' therapy; it is just about being people, meeting for the first time. The skill required here is to be able to listen with an open ear, to talk openly, not to be waiting for the next bit of your theoretical jigsaw to fall into place. Being positively disposed from the outset, as mentioned earlier, helps us with all the other skills required.

I often get people on training courses to imagine that they are at a bus stop and the bus has been delayed. They can choose either to sit in silence or to talk. If they talk, what would they say to someone new? How might the conversation go?

2 The ability to explore any pre-session change

One of the beliefs that SF brief therapists hold is that things change, constantly. Throughout my time working with drug and alcohol users and people with enduring mental health problems, I have noticed that things change from month to month, week to week, day to day, and even from minute to minute.

It is useful to establish from the outset of the first meeting whether anything has changed for the client from referral to the point when they are sitting in the room with you. This can give the therapist clues to the client's capacity to change, and what helps them. This is extremely useful both in the immediacy of the conversation and later. In the immediacy of the conversation it allows us to feed back positives; later it allows us to reflect in the end-of-session feedback whether things are already changing.

Exploring pre-session change also highlights exceptions that can lead to further conversation about those exceptions. Again, the skills here are to actively listen, and to know when to intervene. These are the skills required by all SF brief therapists at all stages of the therapeutic process. Additionally, it takes real skill to 'stick to task' and not to forget about pre-session change. You will see below an example of this. Throughout the book examples will be highlighted using text boxes like this one.

EXAMPLE

I remember seeing a man who had stated at assessment that he drank daily from the time he got up until the time he passed out. At his first meeting, he arrived sober. I asked him how come? His reply was '*It would be taking the piss if I turned up drunk… You wouldn't believe that I wanted to change.*'

So even in that morning he had made some (pre-session) changes. My job was to find out how he had managed to do this and what had helped. By making these changes, even in the short term, the client told me that he wanted to change and that he had confidence that therapy could help.

---

3 The ability to listen actively for client strengths, resources and skills, and any past or present utilization of those skills

To be an active listener is an art in itself, in all forms of therapy. The role of the SF brief therapist here is to ask the types of open question that prompt the client to talk in a way that then enables the therapist to listen for the strengths, skills and resources. So when one asks about family and friends, or interests, hobbies, employment etc., it is useful to listen for 'clues' about what the client has done and can do, how they cope and have coped, and any clues to their 'uniqueness'.

The active listening for solution stories, amplifying them and repeating them back to a client and not paying so much attention to the negative behaviour and stories, is in its own way a cognitive technique. It can create a 'kind of cognitive crisis' (McLeod, 1998: 150) where the client becomes more attuned to looking for and relating to solutions than to problems. I have found this to be very true and that clients often come into session 2 or 3 and start off by telling me positives without much of a prompt. An example of this was a client who told me that her depression was not getting any better but that she felt now that it might, given time, more therapy and her seeking more support from her family.

A note of caution here is that while it is extremely useful to do this, do not ignore everything else that is said in pursuit of your agenda to listen for what *you* want to listen for. Remember that the client leads in SFBT; a therapist-led agenda is moving away from the central beliefs of the model.

EXAMPLE

Someone with a significant alcohol problem once told me that he used to be a 'fell runner' (running up and down big hills in Northern England), so I spent some time talking to him about this. He told me of the discipline needed to train for a race, how he had set himself targets, allowed himself time to recover, eat well and so on. My response was to ask him what he had done then that might be helpful for him in dealing with his alcohol issues. He then set himself a 'training regime' to deal with his alcohol issues and was very successful.

EXAMPLE

Another client told me that she had a very large extended family, some of whom had been through similar problems with drugs as she had and who were now 'clean'. She started to visit those family members more often and drew strength from them.

4 The ability to elicit from the client a preferred future and co-construct a rich image or narrative of that future

Everyone has a preferred future, and the SF brief therapist needs to encourage the client to visualize this in terms of what will be happening when that future is reached, that is what they will be doing instead of the problem, not simply getting away from the problem.

Here is the main difference between solution focused and problem focused approaches. SFBT seeks to move towards something, a preferred future, whereas problem focused models concentrate on management or movement away from the problem, and hence the work becomes defined by the problem. It is a skill in itself not to get too drawn into the problem present and past. You do not want to ignore it, but at the same time you want to 'steer' the conversation into being one where building solutions is more likely.

Let's take depression as an example. In a problem focused model of responding to depression, the therapist will focus on understanding the roots of the depression, what triggers depressive episodes, how it has progressed, what the barriers to the depression lifting are, and so on. The focus moves on to 'lifting' the depression, managing the depression or moving away from the depression. In short, not being depressed. Not being depressed may seem like an attractive starting point for someone, but the SF brief therapist's role is to explore what happens *after* the depression is gone. What does the future look like? What will be different? What is there that wasn't there when the depression was?

A life without depression had not even been contemplated by one client but once it was, all sorts of possibilities opened up:

Client: Instead of being depressed? I dunno. Not really thought about it. I dunno, really, normal I suppose.

Therapist: OK, so supposed you noticed you were being normal. What would be different?

C: I'd just be normal, you know normal like other people.

T: Mmmm.

C: Busy, not bored.

T: Oh, OK, busy doing what?

C: Anything, something.

T: I wonder what that would be... any ideas?

C: You're not gonna let this go are you [laughs]?

T: I will if you want me to... [pause], so what might you be doing that tells you that you are 'more normal', busy?

C: I'd get a book from the library, then that would mean I'd gone out, I'd been around more people, I could take the book home so I wasn't bored when I was in.

T: Excellent, sounds like a plan. Any idea what sort of book?

C: Gimme a break, I haven't thought that far yet [laughs again].

This opening up of the possibility that a future exists without the problem at all therefore leads, inevitably, to a preferred future, one not tied to the problem past.

Similarly, when working with clients with drug and alcohol related problems, stopping taking drugs or alcohol is not the goal for once that goal is reached, what next? Often the alcohol or drugs take up such a significant part of someone's life that in the absence of the substances, a void is left. It is our job to find out what they will be doing so that there will not be a void. Gentle questions like 'I wonder what you will be able to do with your time when you no longer have to spend the whole day searching for a fix?' can be helpful, or 'So when you have done with the drinking, what do you think you will be doing instead?'

Not having OCD should not be the goal, but finding out what can be done when one's time is not spent with rituals or OCD behaviours is much more important:

C: Oh, I will have so much more time to do the things I want to do.

T: Like what?

C: Get a job, that would be good.

It is the SF brief therapist's role to get people to describe, in detail, what their life will be like. It is a bit like getting directions. The client needs to be able to visualize being where they want to be, and the stages to getting there. Goal setting and the miracle (wonderful) question are the main vehicles for 'seeing' this preferred future – more about these in later chapters.

5 The ability to look for exceptions and differences

When the founders of SFBT first started calling this style of working SFBT, one of the things they noticed (and started investigating) was that there were often 'exceptions' to the problems that people brought to therapy (Berg & Miller, 1992). There were times when the problem was not there, or was at least not so dominant in clients' lives. The Milwaukee team focused on these 'exceptions' rather than looking for the 'root' of the problems, as many therapies do. They learnt that when they found exceptions they would focus on them even more, getting clients to describe what was working, what was helping, what was different about the times when exceptions were present. This has remained central to SFBT.

There is a real skill to the SF brief therapist noticing these exceptions in clients' stories, for often the clients skim over them, paying scant heed to them. We have to listen very carefully so as not to miss them. Sometimes clients do not even mention exceptions to start with and we need to go looking a little bit further to find them. Either way, in my experience there are always exceptions to be found.

6 The ability to be able to take a non-expert stance towards the client's experiences and constructs

This is a concept which is much debated in the SF world, and many outside the SF world fail to appreciate the way it is utilized in SFBT. While I have outlined it earlier as one of the 'assumptions', there is a real skill in the actual 'doing' of a non-expert stance.

Put simply, a meeting between an SF brief therapist and a client is one where expertise is shared, not assumed in a hierarchical sense – the worker knows the answer, the client receives the wisdom. So, I know what has been useful and helpful in the past with the questions I have asked others, the person I am seeing knows what has been useful and helpful for them (and others they know), and we learn from each other, hoping to have a useful and helpful conversation.

Working with drug- and alcohol-using clients, my first assumption is that they are resourceful – how else would they manage to keep an (often expensive) addiction/habit going? Working with people with depression, my first assumption is that they have some strengths and resilience in order to get by day to day in what is a tiring, lonely and unhappy existence. Working with people living with anxiety, I genuinely admire their desire to overcome that and be able to sit in front of me. I have no idea what that takes for them to do that never having had anxiety in the way they have. Working with someone with OCD, I am clear that they must be pretty clever to make all the links that they make to organize their thoughts and behaviours. That knowledge will be useful in their attempts to make changes.

I would go further here and state that when we do not accept the client's frames of reference and personal constructs of their experiences and meanings, we will encounter resistance as we try, whether we mean to or not, to impose our agendas on to our clients. De Jong and Berg (2002: 19) are clear that when we draw on clients' frames of reference, 'resistance ceases to be a concern'. We are, after all, trying to build a collaborative and helpful relationship. I actually prefer this assertion than that of many SF brief therapists that there is no such thing as resistance. Once we accept the client's frame of reference (or social construct, if you will), we start to help them look for solutions that are applicable to it.

As an example, I might normally work with a drinker by looking at those times they can spend or have spent away from places where alcohol is consumed. A young gay man that I saw could only meet other young gay men in a local gay pub as the town he lived in had no other opportunities for young gay men to socialize. His between-session task, when we got to it, was *not* to avoid the pub, as that would not have fitted with his expertise of his social situation, but was to suggest to a couple of friends who went there that they organize a social event outside the pub on a Monday evening (when the pub was closed) away from alcohol. His previous experience was always that he associated alcohol with 'being himself' and with his friendships. Once he broke that association, things changed quite quickly in his drinking habits.

7 The ability to utilize the 'miracle (wonderful) question'

The miracle question is a question that focuses the client on a time when their 'problem' has disappeared and have moved, or are moving, towards their preferred future. This will be covered in greater depth later (Chapter 6), but it is often the first thing people say they know about when talking of Solution Focused Brief Therapy. However, it is often misunderstood, often asked wrongly and often is the first hurdle at which novice SFBT practitioners fall. All I will say here is that it is difficult to ask this question without 'going through the motions', but very worth persevering with as it opens up so many avenues.

8 The ability to utilize scaling

This is again covered in depth later (Chapter 5). Many therapists and professionals will have used scaling in one form or another and this is often the intervention in SFBT that people new to the approach find easiest to start with. It is also one of the interventions with which clients feel most at ease. However, there are some significant differences in the use of scaling in SFBT compared to other therapeutic models and different skills are required when using scaling in SFBT.

9 The ability to be sensitive to using 'and' and not 'but'

I am grateful to BRIEF (they were then the Brief Therapy Practice) for first bringing my attention to this nuance. Often when we are talking we do not notice the subtlety of the 'small' words we use, and even a slight change in our choice of words can make a big difference. When someone has been having a really hard time and still turns up to see us, we often articulate our amazement, as encouragement and praise, to those we are seeing:

'Wow, you have all that going on **but** you still managed to get here. Well done.'

What that **can** mean to your client (i.e. what they might hear) is:

'*Your problems are not so great that they stopped you coming.*'

It sounds as though you are belittling or negating the problems they are experiencing or the effort it took them to get to see you. Now, listen in your head to this:

'Wow, you have all that going on *and* you still managed to get here. Well done.'

This is a much more positive response that acknowledges what it took for your client to get here.

10 The ability to be sensitive to using 'how' and not 'why'

Again, a small difference in what we ask can make a big difference in what people hear. To me, 'why' questions can pose a challenge whereas 'how' questions are genuine inquiries. Just say these sentences to yourself out loud, and hopefully you will see what I mean.

'*Why* do you think getting off alcohol is going to be good for you?'
'*How* do you think getting off alcohol is going to be good for you?'

Possibilities open up with the second question for the client to be very descriptive. This is what we are looking for.

'*Why* did you do that?'
'*How* did you do that?'

Possibilities open up with the second question for people to explain and describe their strengths and resources, and the steps they have taken that have been useful.

'How?' or 'How come?' seem better to me than 'Why?', although clearly we all have our own ways of speaking. All I am suggesting here is that the SF brief therapist needs to think about how their questions will be heard by their clients. These small nuances are extremely difficult skills to master as our daily lives are full of 'buts' and 'whys'.

11 The ability to give genuine compliments and praise to a client

Not everyone likes to get praise, which is my only word of caution here. Apart from that note of caution, praise is fantastic. It is so important to tell people that they have done well, to give them credit for their efforts.

Many drug and alcohol users are used to getting 'put downs', being told that they are useless and worse. Many people with depression feel that they are 'worthless'. Many people with anxiety feel they 'cannot' do certain things or are not 'normal'. Many teenagers and young people are used to being seen as a problem group just for being teenagers and I marvel at how quickly and how well teenagers often respond to positive feedback in all walks of life, not just in the therapy room.

We do not give compliments as an SF brief therapist because we are nice people or because we are kind (though I hope we are), but because people often respond well to praise. It is good for clients to start to actively listen to what they are doing well and notice it as it happens from there on. It is also extremely powerful for people to hear compliments and praise from an objective third party because even when they get praise and compliments from those close to them, it is not always 'heard' or believed.

It is essential to 'train' clients through the therapeutic process to look for what is working and what will work, for them to acknowledge it for themselves and to give self-praise, especially when our clients are so used to noticing what is not working. However, it is worth pointing out that giving and accepting praise seems to differ around the world. When American therapists give praise to their clients (as seen in many training videos) there seems to be a ready acceptance that this is a good thing to do. British therapists do not seem to give as much praise in my experience, nor do the clients seem to accept it as readily. Interestingly, at a recent SF conference, I saw at least two SFBT practitioners visibly squirm at praise from colleagues. If we cannot accept it, then it becomes difficult to be genuine in giving it to others.

Part of our job, then, is to help people recognize their own achievements and not focus on their failures. Praise and complements should never be false or patronizing, but genuine, warm, encouraging and based in reality (De Jong & Berg, 2002). In extreme examples, where clients have difficulty in accepting praise for themselves, it is sometimes useful to get them to think outside themselves: 'So, if your friend had managed to get into town when they have anxiety about being around people, how would you let them know they had done well?'

12 The ability to negotiate a task outside therapy that is related to the client's movement towards a preferred future

There are debates in the SFBT world about tasks but I am not going to explore those debates here. It is enough for the reader to know that these debates exist. Some solution focused brief therapists no longer use tasks, some have always used tasks; I find them to be useful tools for clients which is why they have been included in this book.

There is a huge difference between 'task setting' and 'task negotiation', and how the differences are viewed by both therapist and client. What I will say is that where possible tasks should always be negotiated, not 'given' by the therapist, which is more common in some other therapies, for example in Cognitive Behavioural Therapy. I will return to this later. I would also say at this point that 'next small steps' or even client experiments can be 'softer' and more attainable than 'setting goals'. I will explain more in Chapter 7.

Skills in 'ways' of working

The Brief Family Therapy Center, in particular Insoo Kim Berg, developed an acronym for the skills that have been highlighted, or at least for the application of those skills: EARS (De Jong & Berg, 2002).

E – Eliciting exceptions: I have mentioned this already and will explore this further in several places in this book. It is without doubt, one of the main skills the SF brief therapist has to develop – how to look for and find exceptions.
A – Amplifying exceptions: Again, this is explored in more detail later. Once found, exceptions need to be opened up.
R – Reinforcing successes and strengths: This is done throughout the SF meeting, from thanking the person for coming, through to client feedback at the end of the session.
S – Start again. Originally this was meant as a prompt to the therapist to ask 'What else is better?' However, it can apply to so many aspects of the SF brief therapy session. If we get stuck as therapists, it is often useful to start again with the client goals and best hopes as the starting point.

To expand on the above, it is useful again to note that by the very nature of the 'brief' part of SFBT we tend to work with a sharper focus. This does not always mean going quickly, however. We must pay attention to our client's pace and adjust our pace and interventions accordingly.

We must always listen to our clients, acknowledging them, validating their experiences and giving them the responses that let them know we are doing so. This is no different from other therapies and is what I would call 'common currency'. Without doing these things we not only risk losing what therapeutic alliance may already exist (and some does already exist or the client would simply leave), we also risk not being able to build on any existing alliance.

We take notes as we go (not all therapists in other models do this). We write 'key' points, words or phrases down, which is especially useful when it comes to giving feedback at the end of the session. I cannot remember the thousands of words spoken in the therapy hour and if I am to give honest feedback and write accurate case notes I need some prompts.

We try to help people leave therapy sooner, rather than later. The traditional emphasis in the therapeutic world of getting to the 'root of the problem' before being able to move on is not our focus. This is a real skill in the way we work in SFBT. We do not allow ourselves to be distracted into looking for the root of the problem.

We are less concerned with the 'accepted norms' of therapy, such as looking for resistance or avoidance, noting transference and countertransference, noticing levels of eye contact, seat positioning, and so on. Instead, we are more concerned with 'what is helpful' and in establishing that with the client from early on in the relationship. We also 'check in' with a client constantly to ensure that we are still on track.

We are not overly concerned with detailed histories unless of course they highlight strengths and competencies, or it is the first time the client story has been told (Macdonald, 2007).

All of the above points do not mean that we are problem-phobic or past-phobic. Talking about the problem initially is why clients often come to see us, and we learn great things about their coping mechanisms in doing this. Talking about the past gives us opportunities to understand the client better (we can never 'fully' understand them) and to see what they have done in the past that has been useful.

So, now you have an idea of the mindset of the SF brief therapist and the basic skills needed to practise SFBT competently, what else does the SF brief therapist hold dear?

PART 3: QUESTIONS WE ASK OF OURSELVES

Solution focused workers constantly 'check in' on the core beliefs and values of the solution focused approach between, during and after sessions. Some of the questions a solution focused worker asks themselves or the client are as follows and will dominate all the interventions outlined in the chapters to come.

Am I being helpful?

The solution focused brief therapist has but one role, to be as helpful as possible. This means listening, using interventions, asking questions and conversing, all of which, if not helpful for the client, are redundant. This is where the parsimonious nature of the SF founders comes into play. Why ask questions if they are not directly relevant and helpful? I will check over and over about the helpfulness of what I am asking and I will gather feedback as often as possible. Not only does this direct my interventions, but it lets the client know that I am genuinely interested and concerned with being helpful.

What does my client find helpful about what we are doing?

Many models assume that with the 'right' questions asked at the 'right' juncture, all is going well, and if it is not then it is down to some deep-rooted theoretical issue such as 'resistance', 'ambivalence', 'transference', or the like. The SF brief therapist asks questions to determine not only if they are being helpful, but also what it is that they are doing/asking/talking about that is helpful. The SF mantra of doing more of what works features here. If a client tells you that they have found focusing on exceptions (to the problem) to be very helpful, do more of it! Likewise, if the client expresses the view that asking about exceptions is not helpful as they can only think of one, it may be useful to explore that exception and not ask about more.

At the end of most sessions, and certainly at the end of all first meetings, I will ask clients to scale the 'usefulness' of the meeting. This is not to be confused with judging how good I am. From the scale rating, and further discussion of that, I will gauge, along with the client, if I am on the right track. The right track is the one that is most helpful for the client, not the one that my model of therapy tells me I am on or that theory tells me is right.

What could I do differently?

You are the professional; you are getting paid, or are at least trained to be the helpful and helping person. If things do not seem to be going well in the client/therapist meetings, or if there seems to be little progress, it is your role to try something different, a different question for instance. While in some models of helping, a client not answering a question might be seen as avoidance or resistance, the SF assumption is that the client must have a good reason not to answer (yet) and we probably need to try something else.

Sometimes a client simply does not understand the question/intervention, sometimes they do not feel it to be useful or appropriate, sometimes we have said something at the wrong time, or what emerges from our thought processes is not in synchronicity with theirs. It matters less about the reason(s) behind the impasse than that we try to do something else. It is surprising to me, every time I do it, how many times clients will direct me when I ask things like 'What could we talk about that will be more helpful for you?' While I have no 'evidence' explaining why clients find this useful, I strongly suspect it is a combination of the therapist 'stepping down' hierarchically and the client being asked to think for themselves what direction the therapy needs to take.

What are the client's skills, strengths and resources?

If you do not know how the client copes, what skills and strengths they have, what support in respect of family and friends, etc., then it is hopeless to expect them to utilize those things. Sometimes people do not fully appreciate their own competencies and clients can be pleasantly surprised when the SF brief therapist reflects back something that they maybe have not realized themselves. In addition, to be aware of the client's skills, strengths and resources means that you, as a therapist, see people in much more functional ways. It is like a domino effect, the more strengths and skills you and the client see, the more they seem to be found.

What does the client's preferred future look like?

What is it that a client wants to happen that is different from now? If you cannot establish with them where they want to get to, you have little chance of helping them know that they are on their way. I am a great believer in getting people to visualize preferred futures, especially after the miracle/wonderful question. I want to see what they see, or at least understand the reality of their preferred futures from their descriptions. These narratives make 'new' memories so that when people actually experience these changes, they are like old friends, welcome.

How will the client recognize the signs of a preferred future happening?

So once you have established where they want to be (preferred future), the next thing is to establish what are the signs of them being on the right path, what will they notice that tells them they are heading in the right direction? What will other people notice? In short, how will the client know they are heading towards where they want to be in terms of their 'goals'?

How will I and the client know if the sessions are useful?

SF brief therapists do not simply assume that we are working well, that therapy is proving a useful tool for the client and that we are doing all we need to. We ask.

We can ask in a number of ways. Perhaps the simplest is 'Did you find this meeting/last week's meeting useful?' If a client says yes, or no, examine further 'What was most useful?' Or 'What could I/we do to make it more useful?' We need to find out if anything that we talked about in the session has proved useful in their real lives outside therapy. I have often had clients say things (in response to a 'best hopes' question/opening) such as 'I would like some ideas about how I could be more confident' or 'I would like to be able to get out more'. Our role is to 'check in' to see if the therapy meetings are helping to achieve or work towards those things. Put bluntly, is coming to therapy useful?

When and how will the client know it's time to stop coming?

A main underpinning of SFBT is that a client should only come to therapy while it is useful and we are working on the 'focus' established in the first meetings. Open-ended, long-term therapy is to be avoided if at all possible. In addition, in the client-led model that SFBT is, it is much more empowering for the client to have a clear idea of when it is time to stop and to initiate that closure themselves rather than be 'told' by the therapist when it is time to stop and risk feeling abandoned or that the work is not finished. Although I can present no empirical evidence for this, I suspect, based on my experience, that we have less 'returners' to therapy when the client has decided when it is time to stop coming.

Closures, both to individual sessions and to the therapy *per se*, will be examined in more detail in Chapter 8. Suffice to say, it is essential that you and the client have a clear understanding from early on in the therapeutic relationship how you will know it is time to stop coming.

How will others know that things are getting better for the client?

This is perhaps where the family therapy work of the founders of SFBT shows itself. In systemic therapy and systems approaches there is recognition that the client is part of other things, a larger system – family units, social networks, the workplace, and so on. This is also accepted and worked with in SFBT, so questions like 'How would your partner know that coming here has been useful?' are stock questions in SFBT. And in this way the client can 'externalize' the signs of improvement. This is especially useful with mandated clients who often attribute their attendance to an external driver/referrer. So we might ask: 'So you are only here because your social worker asked you to come. I wonder what they might notice after this meeting that tells them that this session was useful?'

'Getting better' or 'improving' are things we ask not only the client to notice. We want them to see if others have noticed improvements too, not least because sometimes people have an idea that they are 'not right' then they are 'right', 'unwell' and then 'well'. There is often a long way to go and the journey can seems an arduous or even unmanageable one. For people to notice differences, for the client's partner or friends to tell them they are 'on the way' can give an added momentum to that journey. One of my clients told me that her husband had commented that she was listening to more music again. This indicated to her that she was feeling more 'herself'. And the man whose workmates told him he seemed 'cheerful today' realized that his getting more sleep was starting to pay dividends on his mood.

RECAP: SKILLS, ASSUMPTIONS AND WAYS OF WORKING

You will now have some idea of the basic skills set utilized by the solution focused brief therapist, the mindset of the therapist when working in this way, and the assumptions underlying the practice of SFBT and how the SF brief therapist views the people they see. This will equip you to better understand the specific skills that are explained and explored in the following chapters.

PERSONAL REFLECTION

Looking at the assumption in SFBT of 'good enough', think of an area of your own life. It might be academic achievement, playing a musical instrument, participating in sports. It could even be personal wealth accumulation. What is your ideal? How far away from that are you now? What are the points along the way that tell you that you are getting there? If you don't get there, what will be good enough?

Let me give you an example. At the point of writing this, I am 47. I have been playing badminton (pairs) for two years in order to keep fit. I would love to be able to play at a national level, which would be my ideal, my perfect future, my 10/10. This will never happen. I am too old and by the time I have been playing long enough to be better, my fitness and coordination will have deteriorated further. So, my 'good enough', the point at which I would be happy, is to be able to play regularly in the 'B' Team of the club I attend (we have three teams). I currently captain the C Team and have had a few games with the B Team, so I am well on the way to my 'good enough'.

TRY THIS

The next time you are with a client try being a 'detective'. Whenever a client makes a statement ('I used to work in a baker's, I was a pastry cook'), after your meeting, or during if you can, jot down all the things that this could mean in a positive light about this person, such as: they were able to get to work, they were organized, they can cook, they know about timing, they know maths (mixing ingredients), and so on.

KEY TERMS USED IN THIS CHAPTER

Skills, listening, differences, noticing, assumptions, strengths, good enough, how, being helpful, utilization, strengths, signs, EARS, what works.

SUGGESTED FURTHER READING

Macdonald, A. (2007). *Solution-focused therapy: theory, research and practice*. London: Sage.

This is one of the most accessible, comprehensive books about SFBT I have read. It manages to give a depth to the history, roots and theoretical assumptions underpinning SFBT, while at the same time detailing the extent of research and exploring the breadth of SF approaches.

O' Connell, B. (1998). *Solution-focused therapy*. London: Sage.
Bill O' Connell has a way of writing that simplifies often complex things. This book is a good read and covers a broad range of areas. A useful book in its entirety, I would direct the reader to the very useful table on page 21 which shows the difference between problem-focused and solution-focused approaches.

3

OPENINGS IN SFBT AND THE ROLE OF THE THERAPIST

LEARNING OUTCOMES

By the end of this chapter the reader will:

- Understand the importance of focused openings in Solution Focused Brief Therapy
- Be clear about the role of the therapist in SFBT
- Appreciate the importance of exploring pre-session change
- Understand how to use problem-free Talk in an SF way
- Understand the importance of highlighting strengths skills and resources in an SF opening

---

Common practice and guidelines dictate that therapists and other helping profession-als plan significant pieces of work with clients, using such tools as assessment and care planning; only to sometimes not see those plans come to fruition as clients can stop coming at any time and for any number of reasons. This can be at the very least frus-trating for the professional and can be unhelpful for the client. The SF brief therapist does not assume that any session is more or less likely to lead to subsequent sessions. Therefore it is important that each SFBT session is self-contained in that it has a beginning, a middle and an end.

In the first session (and subsequent sessions) openings are extremely important. Openings should be respectful and the start of the session's focus: they set the scene for the client and therapist to be future-focused, solution-oriented and responsive to the client's needs. We establish a strong therapeutic alliance quickly by being responsive to client agendas and truly listening to what they want to achieve by seeing us, not by fitting them into some category of work to be done according to a rigid approach. When a therapeutic relationship is established at an early stage, it may be a good indicator of a positive outcome (Bachelor & Howarth, 1999).

If we start the therapeutic process in a structured and focused way, we are much more likely to keep to that. If we do not, then we have to work very hard to get back or maintain a focus for the work and we end up meandering away from the focus. The role of staying focused starts from the very beginning; the first openings are paramount to being a good SF brief therapist. De Shazer likened the SF therapist to Sherlock Holmes, listening for clues and not being distracted by red herrings that lead to less useful paths that distract us from the focus of the work (de Shazer, 1994). Interestingly, I attended a workshop at a conference where Bill O'Connell and his associates presented highway signs that could be associated with SFBT. To keep our focus, they showed us a diversion sign, with the message of not being diverted from the client's best hopes.

When I facilitate training I often observe that those from the helping professions spend a significant amount of time making people feel 'at ease'. There is nothing wrong in this at all although what can happen is that people go off on tangents that do not focus on the task in hand. So please carry on making people feel at ease, but always bear in mind that you are there for a purpose, and you can still help people to feel at ease while retaining focus.

It is important that once the therapist and client have agreed on a focus for the therapeutic intervention, the therapist must be disciplined and not search for meanings outside that focus, or the client's definition of what that focus is. To do this could lead the therapist to detract from the client's agenda and to lose sight of the agreed goals (Koss & Shiang, 1994). So, if the client's stated goals or best hope is to gain more confidence as a result of coming to see you, in a solution focused approach an examination and exploration of how they (and others) will know when they are more confident is much more applicable than an exploration of what has happened to them many years ago (possibly which led to a lack of confidence). They have stated that they want to be more confident, not that they want to understand why they are not so confident.

Clients may have had assessments and pre-intervention questionnaires and various interventions before coming to see you. While one must not ignore what has gone before (especially in relation to risk), it is worthwhile remembering that you are seeing someone for the first time and should not be unduly influenced by the process of assessment(s). Generally, assessments are full of problem focused questions and assumptions. Assessments are not wholly factual but are influenced by either the client's mood at that moment in time or by another professional's thinking at any given moment in time.

I remember asking a client on entering a therapy room how they were coping with their presenting problem and their response was that they thought they were doing OK until they had filled out 'those depressing forms'. They were talking about a well-known self-assessment tool for depression and anxiety. There are exceptions, and certainly the Solution Focused Measure of Occupational Function (Duncan, Ghul & Mousley, 2007) is one to be held up. This assessment utilizes positively framed statements as opposed to how entrenched their problems may be.

That being said, even within the problem-saturated assessment processes found in many settings, the solution focused worker can work some magic. Hopefully, the next few paragraphs will give a taste of what CAN be done. To give you an example, a well-known self-assessment tool asks how many days of the week a client is 'bothered' by feelings of anxiety. This is asked to determine how invasive these feelings are in a client's life. The solution focused brief therapist does not disregard this, but focuses on the times when the anxiety is less invasive. So, if a client answers that anxiety bothers them for at least three days per week, the SF brief therapist should instantly think 'I wonder what they are doing on the other days that is helpful'. Not only will they think this, they will ask this.

As another example, a drink diary I once saw asked the client to list all the days that they had been drinking alcohol. They also had to list feelings before using, feelings after using, reasons for using and problems associated with the use of alcohol on that day. They then came to see me in an absolutely miserable mood. I visibly tore up the drink diary and we worked together on a different diary which had the following headings:

- The days I managed to do something else instead of drinking
- How I felt after I had managed a drink-free day
- What or who helped me
- My point on a scale out of 10, in terms of confidence of beating my 'booze demon' (these were his words for his issues with alcohol)

This therapist 'shift' from focusing on what is working, rather than what is problematic generally encourages the client to also think about the times when the problem is reduced or not there. So our role is to:

- Listen to clues
- Listen for exceptions (and amplify them)
- Ask useful questions persistently and at the same time gently
- Listen actively for any strengths and unique coping strategies we hear
- Listen for past successes and future strategies
- Collaborate with the client on their agenda, their ways forward and their preferred future
- Above all, our role is to stick to task.

In my opinion SFBT is truly client-centred. McLeod (1998) states that person-centred therapy has an understanding that people have a view of how they are and of how they would like to be. SF brief therapists share this view and help people to harness their own uniqueness in moving forward to their preferred future. The active role of the SF brief therapist here is to direct the client more towards that preferred future with gentle questioning and enquiries. This means that we anticipate the discovery of strengths and resources and capabilities by such a line of questioning. In a personal conversation with Bill O'Connell, he once said to me that our role was to be the 'benevolent enquirer'. This struck a chord with me.

All of this focus and clarification (both internally and externally) of role starts with the opening questions; if we get them wrong, we are for ever struggling to regain the focus. This is where many therapists new to the SFBT approach start to go wrong – at the beginning.

When I train others in the approach, I deliberately break down the interventions and 'parts' of the therapy session into components, with the openings being dealt with as 'stand alone' parts of the model. If we do not pay due attention to the openings, we are often tempted, as previous training and experience (of our problem-saturated world) will encourage, to move into problem solving and helping, as we do successfully in those parts of our lives that are not being the therapist, often assuming we know what is best. We must assume no such thing when in the role of solution focused brief therapist.

Openings are not just greetings. We should not underestimate their potency in ensuring that the rest of the therapeutic time is most useful for the people we are seeing.

INTRODUCING SALLY

Sally is going to feature as I talk about each intervention in this book. This is because I saw Sally for a relatively long time in terms of my usual solution focused practice – 23 sessions over nearly 18 months. The average number of sessions per client in the department of psychology where I worked, both as a paid locum and as a volunteer, over nine years was 5.3 sessions.

Sally referred herself to me after her doctor suggested she 'needed' counselling. She was certainly not convinced that seeing me would be helpful. Rather, she was sure that nothing could help and that she was (even though she was only in her mid thirties) just waiting for death to come.

Sally was an extremely active young woman. Only two years before coming to see me she had cycled around Europe and parts of Asia with her husband, playing a fiddle along the way, busking to help fund her two-year adventure. Ten months prior to our first meeting she had gone into hospital for a routine operation and contracted a post-operative infection that nearly killed her. In fact she was left quite severely disabled and could no longer walk unaided (she had a leg brace and now used a stick), she had lost a lot of movement in her left hand, especially the fingers, and she lived in constant pain from a tracheotomy. She no longer enjoyed 'anything'. Music, which was her life, along with travel held no joy for her and she had no realistic hope of her physical situation improving. She had enjoyed a close and intimate relationship with her husband and told me at our first meeting that they had not had any sexual contact since the operation. She also told me that he was kind and patient and was her 'rock'.

You will read more of Sally later.

OPENING QUESTIONS

In the UK and many other areas in the world, therapists are required to outline the confidentiality limitations of the organization in which they work to clients before the start of therapy, how their information will be recorded and stored, their access to that information, and so on. They may also be required to outline how they are going to work with a client, providing a short explanation of the therapeutic model, for instance. There may well be a requirement to explain what will happen should risks be identified, such as suicidal ideation. Finally, there may be a 'policy' to explain health and safety issues, such as where the fire exits are.

After all these things are done it is time to start the work proper, as it were. The reason that these issues have been highlighted before talking about 'openings' is two-fold: First, 'openings' are not therapeutic at first, but practical, and this places different demands on the professional than simply being the therapist. Secondly, it is to demonstrate that a 'shift' is required before the therapeutic opening questions. Once the practicalities are out of the way, I often mark this by saying something like: 'Are you ready to get started?' or 'Are you comfortable to begin the meeting now?', or even 'OK that's the practicalities dealt with, are you all right for us to start the therapeutic work?'

Example Question 1: 'What do you hope to get from today's session?'

This is a great opener. Rather than a woolly 'Let's see where we go' start, we immediately help the client focus on what will be helpful in the next hour, 50 minutes or whatever time we have, in relation to what might happen when they leave the session.

By saying 'from' today's session rather than 'in' today's session, we are recognizing straight away that people will take something from the session outside into their real lives. They will not simply leave it in the therapy room where it may not be useful other than in the therapy room. We may need to 'home in' on the client's responses to ensure this is the case as we do not simply assume that people take things away. In fact, I have often heard people say they are working on things 'in therapy'. I'd rather they were working on things outside therapy. People may say things like: 'I want to get off heroin, don't I?' As this is unlikely to happen in the course of the next hour, an appropriate response might be something like: 'And if this meeting were to help you to start to do that, what do you think would be useful to do/talk about here?' or 'Supposing something started here to help you get off of heroin, what might you notice that is different between the end of this meeting and the next time we meet?'

We also need to establish at this point that 'getting off heroin' is but one goal on the way to doing something else. If the absence or management of a problem is the goal, then we are tied to the problem – we are problem focused. The solution focused brief therapist needs to find out what will be happening instead of the problem, or what will be happening *after* the problem has gone. This becomes the focus, and it needs to be established early on.

> *Therapist:* What do you hope to get from today's session?
> *Client:* I don't want to be hiding away anymore.
> *T:* So if you are not hiding away, what would you be doing *instead* of hiding away?
> *C:* Doing things, going shopping, going into town, you know, normal things.

Another two opening questions you could try are as follows.

Example Questions 2 and 3

> Q. 2 What are your best hopes *for* today?

or

> Q. 3 What are your best hopes *from* today?

Here are two questions with just a single word difference but they can have quite different meanings. Neither is better than the other but the answer you may get may be quite different.

As with the first question, these questions start to focus on what the client wants. The first of these two interventions, 'What are your best hopes *for* today?', sets the framework firmly in the 'here and now'. A client might respond to this question something like: 'For you to understand what I am going through.' We might respond by asking how they would know that we had more understanding, how having that understanding would be helpful for them, and so on.

In solution focused work, it is not inappropriate to ask about what may happen 'in' the session because the session itself is not the focus – the 'future focus' is the focus. This means that the client may well respond to what they want *you* to do, or what they want to achieve *in* the session, such as 'getting things off their chest', 'talking' or being 'listened to'.

These are certainly the aims of many people entering the therapy room for the first time. In some ways this part of developing the therapeutic alliance by listening to clients' stories is common currency in any therapeutic relationship, and a strong therapeutic alliance seems to be an essential part of a positive outcome to therapy for clients (Lambert et al., 1992). The skill is when to switch from listening to the problems to focusing on preferred futures. Listening to the problems that the client has to tell us *is* important, and we must never ride roughshod over clients, although this does not set a future focus or set a clear understanding of the time spent outside the therapy room being more important.

If asking question 2, you may need to 'home in' further later. This is OK. Some therapists' styles are less focused and more relational in the beginning of the therapeutic relationship. They will need to know how and when to switch to a more future focused set of questions. Some SF brief therapists prefer to start with a more minimalist and focused version of the question, which is the second of the two questions.

By saying 'What are your best hopes *from* today?', the focus is immediately on the future, and that future is outside the therapy room. Here I must pay due deference to BRIEF for their many online and face-to-face discussions which have clarified this difference for me. For example, the client may answer: 'Well, I want to get better and feel more at ease around my work colleagues.' From this we can begin to ask how they would know that their time in the session was helping them towards those aims. How would others know? What would they and others notice? What does feeling 'more at ease' mean to them? What does it 'look like'?

Other ways of opening a meeting could be to ask:

> 'What are your best hopes for coming here?'
> 'How will you know if seeing me is being helpful?'
> 'If, on leaving today, this session has been useful, what would have happened?'
> 'How will your partner/friends/parents know that it was useful for you to come here?'

All are variations on a theme; all are carefully worded to ensure that clients focus on what is being helpful in working with the therapist and how the work is moving towards the preferred future. A personal favourite question of mine is:

> 'How will you know if today has been of use to you? What might happen after this meeting? What will you or others notice that is different?'

From this question we can elicit from the client what they might do after seeing us. This is crucial, for their life outside the therapy room is where they will make the changes. In the session they will think about what might be different, and then, hopefully, they will actively look for this after they have left. A really useful interjection after an initial answer is a stock favourite in the SF world: 'And what else?' This can be asked several times to encourage the client to expand on their original answer.

We might follow this opening exchange by confirming with the client that when their goal is reached, that is time to stop coming: 'So when you are able to do that, go into town on your own, is that when our work together will be done, when it is time to stop coming?' There is more about closures later in this book, but it is useful to know here that establishing a focus for the work also means establishing a focus for when the work stops. Solution Focused Brief Therapy is not open-ended or continuous in relation to ever-presenting issues. Once someone has been successful in reaching the goals they came to you with, or at least reached an agreed point towards those goals, it is time to stop.

And we could also ask: 'How will others know if today (or coming to therapy in general) has been of use to you?' This question gets the client to think about others, and gives them an idea of what observable changes people might see that tells them things are getting better. There is little doubt that this question originated from somewhere in (systemic) family therapy, as the original 'founders' of SFBT were initially family therapists and/or social workers. This question can not only be used to elicit from the client how significant others will notice changes, but can also be used very successfully with 'mandated' clients, that is those who are sent to us as part of a legal or other requirement.

Mandated clients often appear initially to have little investment in a change process other than to keep their probation officer, social worker, youth offending worker 'off their back'. While we do not challenge or agree with this focus (we do not take sides), we might explore how the referrer will know that the client seeing us has been useful. These clients may not immediately want to engage with the therapy or therapist. In fact, they are often quite hostile to the process. So to ask them what others would see as a useful goal, set of goals or even just time spent with the therapist allows engagement by proxy as it were, a starting place.

The above interventions/questions are not always the very first words out of a therapist's lips. Indeed, to ask them without any of the societal niceties may seem a little abrupt and harsh, though they are useful questions to ask in the first few minutes of meeting the client.

It is also useful in these opening exchanges to look for any pre-session change that may have occurred, especially if it highlights the client's strengths, skills and resources. So now you are aware that the role of the therapist in the opening exchanges is to establish a focus for the work to be done and to relate it to the client's life outside the therapy room, what next?

SALLY

As mentioned earlier, I will illustrate each intervention with how Sally and I worked together. Here are our opening exchanges:

Therapist: Hi Sally, I see from your notes that your GP thought it might be a good idea for you to come and see me. Have you had any thoughts about what would make coming to see me useful for you?

Sally: Nothing can be useful really, I'm not going to get better. I'm only really coming here because the doctor suggested it. He's been really good with me and I didn't want to let him down, so I'm here, but no, I'm not really sure.

T: Oh, OK, so you are not convinced that coming here can be useful to you?

S: No, ... I mean, look at me. I'm not going to get better [*she points to her leg and the brace on it, motions to her stick and then puts her hand forward so that I can see that her little finger and the one next to it are stiff and curled slightly*]. Nothing you can say is going to change that is it?

T: No, you're right, I cannot change those things. Nor can you from what I have read and what you have said. Your physical situation is tough to say the least, and it is no wonder that you are 'low in mood' to use your doctor's words. So, I wonder what on earth made your doctor think coming here could be useful?

S: I think he thinks it will help my mood, make me feel better. I'm not so sure about that. I'm pretty much all talked out about it really.

T: So, if he saw that your mood had lifted and that you felt a little better, he would feel that your coming here was useful [*pause*]?

What is important here is that I am not challenging Sally's thoughts or feelings, just not going with them at the moment. Instead I am concentrating on trying to establish some goals for Sally coming to see me.

(Continued)

(Continued)

S: Yes, but I'm not sure about that at all, I've tried everything and it really [pause], well there's no point.

T: Yep, I guess I'd be feeling a bit … or a lot … like that too. Even though you feel like that, you have somehow made the effort to come today, and at the very least make a start. I have to admire that in you, and hope I can do justice to that effort that you have made.

Sally did seem a little bewildered at this statement. Some months later she said that she was surprised at my use of words. She felt they were 'old-fashioned', but nice, what we call in the UK a 'backhanded compliment'.

I am going to leave Sally at this point. She was very down and had little idea of what she wanted or believed could happen in therapy, yet, she had turned up. She had engaged and she was clear what others would see would be useful 'for' her. As an opening this gave me something to go on, though, as you will see later, it took some time for her to accept that she had any goals for herself. Here is where the pace of the therapist (myself) needed to match her pace and go slowly, intervening with appropriate questions at appropriate moments.

PROBLEM—FREE TALK

Problem-free talk is used in many therapeutic models and in many ways and at many points in the therapeutic contact. The same is true for problem-free talk in SFBT though it is explored in this chapter as it often flows naturally from the openings or certainly around that point in the meeting. That being said, it will drift in and out of the time spent between therapist and client quite naturally, and I would assert here that this is a good thing as we want the meetings to be focused, of course, and we also want them to be client led. This may mean that we will 'allow' a level of client meanderings. It is our job to reflect on the usefulness of these meanderings with the client, and the usefulness of problem-free talk should never be underestimated.

It might be useful to explain here what I mean by problem-free talk as one practitioner said to me recently 'All of SFBT is problem-free talk'. He was right to a large degree (thanks Greg), and certainly many SF interventions are problem-free talk. What I mean here is the deliberate use, by the therapist, of engaging in general conversation for the purposes outlined below.

Problem—free talk is essential for many reasons

Problem-free talk is any talk that is not about the client's presenting problem. It aids the therapeutic alliance if the therapist is genuinely interested in the client and the client knows this. It also breaks down the hierarchical therapist/client construct if we simply 'talk' for a while. SFBT differs from other therapies in the level of disclosure permitted (Macdonald, 2007; O'Connell, 2007). Not that we disclose personal details, or any problems that we may have, but it is certainly permissible to discuss shared interests, hobbies, and so on. If nothing else, it means that we do not put ourselves on a pedestal as the therapist, and that we are trying to have a helpful conversation, free of hierarchical constraints and not simply impart some guarded wisdom. To maintain a blank canvas of not knowing or sharing anything seems to me to be unhelpful in developing an alliance or being a collaborator in therapy. I remember when I first did some counselling training and was told that if a client ever asked anything about you, you were to answer, 'This session is about you not me'. This is not a good way to enhance the therapeutic alliance in my opinion and comes from a tradition in therapy that is more hierarchical and guarded than SFBT. I see no reason not to respond in less guarded ways, even if you are not going to answer a direct question. For instance, if a parent says to me, 'With small kids you never get a minute to yourself. Can you understand what that is like?', I could say 'I can imagine', or I could say 'Yes, it can certainly be demanding'. The latter tells the client that I have had small children and understand, to some degree, their statement more than just 'imagining' what it is like. To me, this can only aid the alliance. However, this level of disclosure must always be for a reason like this. We must never, in my opinion, expand such an answer so that the focus shifts from client to therapist. A simple rule of thumb is to ask yourself before disclosing anything 'How is this going to be helpful for the client?'

When I am introducing myself and the way I work to people, I will say something like:

'And I will be asking you quite a lot of questions. You do not have to answer them, or you may not want to answer them at that point. That is fine, just let me know. Equally, you are free to ask me questions. Like you, I may choose not to answer them and I will always try to tell you why.'

Problem-free talk is a good way of discovering the client's skills, strengths and resources. I facilitated a short workshop at a conference recently on this very topic and developed an acronym for why we utilize problem-free talk – SHUSH:

Shows the client that you are listening
Highlights any strengths, skills, resources and exceptions
Understanding of the client's unique being starts to happen
Strengthens the therapeutic alliance
Hierarchy becomes less apparent, thus collaboration is easier.

Genuine praise during problem-free talk is not to be shied away from. For instance, a client who is depressed may feel pretty low, but that should not stop you expressing astonishment that they used to be a marathon runner, or that they have managed to raise two children.

There are exceptions. Some clients find it very difficult to accept or even acknowledge praise. In some cases, such as when I worked with a young woman with Body

Dysmorphic Disorder, praise may be just too challenging and even damaging in the therapeutic process. Tread carefully and 'adapt' the level of praise to that which sits comfortably with the client.

Most therapeutic models employ problem-free talk. In SFBT the main purpose is clear: it is an opportunity to listen for strengths, resources and exceptions (to the 'problem'). I use the term 'listen for' rather than 'look for' as we need to hear these things as they occur naturally; to go looking for them means we are being therapist-led. I am grateful to BRIEF (again), in particular to Chris Iveson, for clarifying my thoughts on this matter. So, somehow, we need to start to engage in this problem-free talk. It is not always easy as of course clients come to us with problems. Here are some suggestions:

> T: So this is the first time we have met. I know a little of why you are here from what you have just told me about your best hopes, but I know very little about you other than that. Can you please tell me a little about yourself, your family, what you like doing, etc.?

Or

> T: Hi X, I have read your referral form and I have some idea of what has been going on for you, though it doesn't say much else about you, like your hobbies, interests, social networks, what you like, who you are. Can you fill in some gaps for me please?

Encourage the client to view their life as a whole, remembering that although they are a drinker or a drug user or depressed or anxious, they may also be a competent parent, a musician, hold down a job, have friends, have interests and hobbies. This makes them more of a whole person than simply what they bring in terms of the 'problem'.

By doing this we can externalize the issue/problem that they have brought to therapy and see it as a part, not the whole, of their life. This enquiring intervention also shows the client that you are interested in them and thus helps to build a therapeutic alliance.

With some more reticent clients you might even play a game of 'I'll ask a question of you, and then you ask one of me'. A real example of this was when a particularly shy young man came to see me with confidence problems and drinking issues.

CASE EXAMPLE: A YOUNG MAN WHOSE BEST HOPES WERE TO BE MORE CONFIDENT WITHOUT HAVING TO DRINK SO MUCH

Therapist: OK David, now we know what you want to achieve, I wonder if you wouldn't mind telling me something about you, so I might get to know you a bit better. SO, what do you like doing mostly?

Client: What do you mean?

T:	Well, do you watch TV, like music, sport, reading, you know? Is there anything that interests you?
C:	Yeh, I like music, mostly rap, hip hop, a bit of metal.
T:	Right, what sort of rap, oh, sorry, your turn to ask me.
C:	Do you like rap then?
T:	Actually, I do like some, especially early stuff like Sugar Hill Gang and Grandmaster Flash … some newer stuff, but not the real 'gangsta' stuff. It gets a bit boring. I like more west coast, you know, stuff with a tune.
C:	That old stuff is like, quite funny. Didn't put you down as a rap fan…
T:	Never said I was a fan, just said I liked SOME of it.

[*Both laugh*]

OK, from this we had the start of a conversation, and I found out later that David (not his real name) did not get drunk when he went to town to buy new music, whereas he used alcohol to cope with most other situations where he might come into contact with people. This exception was explored. He could interact with the staff in the music shop well. He had a knowledge base and they had a shared interest, so his confidence in these situations was heightened, though he had not realized this until we had had this conversation. He went on to look at other exceptions, such as when he went to a 'convention' with a friend.

David realized, from our very first meeting, that there were times when he already felt more confident and did not need to drink, and these times were directly related to him 'being on a mission' or, in other words, having a clear purpose and the knowledge and skills to fulfil that purpose. This realization may not have happened without some general discussion that was not directly related to the 'problem'.

Even if a client cannot think of anything to talk about in a problem-free way (this is very rare if the therapist works in a sensitive and enquiring way), you can comment on them being able to get to the appointment: 'Right, so all of this is going on, and you still managed to get here. That must have taken some effort. Well done.'

Sometimes, clients may want to talk in problem-free ways but are not ready to do so immediately. This is fine, we should not force the issue. Rather, we should wait until an opportunity arises to intervene with some problem-free talk, remembering that the client does not 'know' our way of working or our 'script'. Their construct may be that to come and see a therapist means talking about problems and negative feelings. We need to respect that. It should be noted here that 'solution talk' or 'solution finding' is talking in a problem-free way, but the explicit use of problem-free talk is a little different.

Strengths in problem-free talk

People come to therapy often expecting to tell the story of their problem. A good solution focused worker will not try to hurry people along, but rather will listen to the story and look for clues or 'leaders' to the next piece of the conversation. Most SF brief therapists would accept SFBT is a strength–based model and would actively listen for and amplify strengths as part of the work.

There are exceptions and BRIEF would say that to spend time *looking* for strengths can detract from the client-led agenda and that by concentrating on this we might miss something. I tend to agree. To me, the difference here is between 'listening for' and 'looking for', as mentioned earlier. In SFBT we listen with the ear of a detective. We filter out that which is not needed to be helpful and home in on what is useful and helpful. When we hear strengths, we note them.

In actively listening for strengths, skills and resources, we have to know what to do when we find them (and we will). That is, we have to amplify these strengths, skills and resources and find out how they might be applicable when dealing with the presenting issue and hopes for a future where the presenting issue is not there, or is reduced.

CASE EXAMPLE: A DEPRESSED CLIENT WITH LOW–SELF ESTEEM

Client: I don't do anything much, watch telly mostly.
Solution Focused Reflection: What do you enjoy watching on the telly (TV)?

From this, the worker can learn more of the client's interests and lead into other discussion of current or previous interests outside watching TV. This can in turn lead to insights into strengths, skills and resources that the client may utilize. It may also lead to descriptions of a less problem-saturated past or present.

T: What do you enjoy watching on the telly?
C: I don't like soaps or much daytime telly, but I do like those 'do up your house' programmes, and I don't mind a decent documentary.
T: Oh, by 'do up your house' programmes do you mean when someone comes in and does it or gives you tips on how to do it yourself?
C: Both really, but I like it when they show me how to do stuff. That means I don't have to pay much, 'cause I am short most of the time [*does not have much money*]. I only get my benefits. Yeah, they're good....
T: And do you do stuff you learn on the programmes?
C: Sometimes, when I feel up to it.
T: Can you, um, give me an example?
C: What do you mean, I don't get it, sorry.
T: Sorry, I should have explained that better. Can you give me an example of something you have done in the house after watching one of these programmes?
C: Oh right, like when I changed a washer on the tap instead of letting it drip?
T: Wow, yep, spot on. Tell me about that [*laughs*]. I might learn something myself.

This established the fact that the client had skills and was praised for those skills. It also puts the therapist (me) one step down from being an 'expert' by acknowledging that the client has skills that the therapist may not have. It also transpired that this client checked out on the internet the type of washer he needed, where it was sold and then went and bought it from a shop, showing that he was more confident in this instance. It is amazing how a seemingly innocuous question such as what a client watches on TV can lead to such useful paths for both therapist and client to take. This is another illustration that by following the client's lead, we, as SF brief therapists, can be directed in our work and not retreat to the safety of therapist-led formulations. Our formulations are responsive to the client's lead and are not pre-planned.

CASE EXAMPLE: A FEMALE CLIENT PRESENTING WITH ANXIETY AND PANIC ATTACKS

Client: I used to like gardening.
Solution Focused Reflection/Intervention: When you did more gardening, what did your garden look like?

Here is an opportunity to help the client visualize something that was/is important to her which may be helpful in moving her towards her stated goals. At this point I may not be sure of how helpful it will be, but as the client has mentioned it, I follow her lead.

T: When you did more gardening, what did your garden look like?
C: Well, not the bloody mess it is now. I'm ashamed to look at it. The neighbours must wonder why I've let it go, but I can't go out there and I can't tell them about all this, can I? I mean, it's right embarrassing and I'd panic about even trying to tell them.
T: OK, supposing, just supposing… that you were a little better and was able to go in the garden for, say, no more than five minutes. What would be the first thing you would notice that tells you that maybe there was a small improvement to both you and the garden?
C: I don't think I could go out there. What if next door saw me and wanted to talk? No, I just couldn't.
T: OK, I'm not saying you have to. I'm just saying, *IF* you could, just imagining for the moment, not 'doing'.
C: Er, I'd er, clean some of the leaves off the patio, they look a right mess, or…., yeh, the leaves first, put them in the compost bin….
T: OK, so that would make it look a bit tidier then?

(Continued)

(Continued)

C: Yeah, I suppose I could do that. It would only take a couple of minutes with a dustpan and brush.

T: Oh, I see, from just imagining, it sounds like you *are* going to do this then. Have I got that right? Even though your neighbour might come out?

C: Well it's a start and I can always go back in if he comes out. Mind you, he doesn't much go out when it's cold anyway.

T: So, it sounds like you have the start of an idea there.

From this small step, which we agreed as a between session task (more of this later, in Chapter 7), the client started to do something within her perceived capabilities. It was hard enough to be a challenge, but small enough to be 'doable'. After this, the garden became a 'theme' and we developed a shared understanding about the plants, weather, planning, hard work, time, etc., with her finishing therapy when she was able to visit the garden centre alone.

CASE EXAMPLE: SELF-ESTEEM ISSUES

Client: I go out with my mates, that sort of thing.
Solution Focused Reflection: You have people who like you. Do you think that they may be potential sources of support in what you are trying to achieve?

This young man wanted to go to college to get more of an education though was 'scared' that as he had left school some six years earlier with few qualifications he would not be able to go. It transpired that one of his friends was taking evening classes at the local college and had some contacts. This proved to be very supportive.

We might also look at what family people have locally. It is very rare that someone has absolutely no friends or family, although where this is the case we would look at who they *do* interact with – shopkeeper, doctor, you, etc. Family and friends can be as useful in someone getting better as when they are supporting them when they are unwell or have a problem. Use them, or rather, get the client to use them.

Even the most 'difficult' answers can have some unexpected results:

CASE EXAMPLE: AGORAPHOBIA, SOCIAL PHOBIA, DEPRESSION

Client: I spend most of my day in bed.
Solution Focused Reflection: What do you do with your time when you manage to get up?

Here we are exception finding again. The client said 'most of my day…', so I was interested in the exceptions to this and what we could learn from them that could be applied elsewhere. When the client answered that they only got up to go to the toilet or to cook, I discovered that they actually ate reasonably healthily and cooked well – their own effort to combat the fact that they were not getting any exercise. We talked about where they had learned to cook, how they managed to eat so healthily on a limited budget, and so on.

When a woman tells me 'I'm just a mum and housewife', I make the assumption that she has time management skills, organizational skills, an awareness of health and safety, nutrition, and so on. I will then home in on these skills and exceptions, if only to highlight them to the client.

So, using problem-free talk is useful in that we hear things from a client that have been, or are currently, useful and helpful. This becomes even more important later in the therapeutic work when we can reflect on the time spent using problem-free talk to establish, confirm and utilize discovered skills for future solution building.

SALLY

T: So now you are not working and spend a lot of time at home [*she had told me this*], what do you do with yourself? How do you keep yourself occupied? What do you enjoy doing?

S: Not much really. I clean the house best I can, get tea ready for Mick [*her husband*], stare out the window, cry. I don't enjoy anything. I can't do anything I used to do.

T: Sounds pretty tough and it must be a real chore to even motivate yourself to clean and cook. What did you used to do, then, before your injuries?

S: I played music every day. I've played the fiddle, well classical violin first, since I was a kid. I can't do that now, my fingers won't work it well enough. We were always going away, took our bikes, I've even had to let my sister have the dog because I can't take him for long walks [*starts to cry*].

T: I'm sorry, that sounds so hard for you. Is there anything you do or have tried to do that makes you feel a little bit better at all?

S: No, I've tried everything. TV is just depressing. I can't bear to listen to music now. I just spend my days waiting for Mick to come home.

T: And is it any better then, when Mick comes home?

S: He sometimes cheers me up a bit, but most of the time he doesn't. I just pretend he does so he doesn't feel bad all the time seeing me like this, but it's not real. It would devastate him to know how bad I feel. If it wasn't for him and my morals and my faith I would have ended it by now, but I could not do that to him. We've been together through so much.

(Continued)

(Continued)

Time to leave Sally again. On the face of it, the problem-free talk was not problem-free. She was problem-saturated, and little wonder. However, with a solution focused ear what I heard was:

- She is choosing to stay alive
- She cooks
- She cleans
- Music is/was important
- She has supportive family
- She wants to maintain a façade of being well for someone she cares about
- She has tried some things
- She has strong morals and faith
- She cares about others still (dog to sister).

It was important to note all of these things at the time, and I did, in her case notes, as some come into play later with Sally. What is important to note is that while Sally was very problem focused in this meeting (as might I have been), the SF brief therapist skills of listening with an SF ear had already been utilized to start viewing competencies, skills, resources and exceptions.

RECAP: OPENINGS IN SFBT AND THE ROLE OF THE THERAPIST

So we have established that the SF brief therapist needs to clarify the following things in their first meeting:

- What does the client want to achieve as a result of coming to see you?
- What the focus of the work will be and when it will finish.

The therapist also needs to establish an alliance, use problem-free talk, listen for exceptions, and be vigilant to the client's strengths, skills and resources.

PERSONAL REFLECTION

Do I wander off topic with clients? Do I establish a clear focus? If not, how do I get back on track? What do I, as the professional, need to do or ask or talk about that will help me and the client find a focus for the work we are to do together? How will I and the client know we have done this?

TRY THIS

The next client you see for a first time, when you are writing up notes, use subheadings (in this order):

- Client's best hopes from our work
- Problem-free talk
- Client's strengths, skills and resources
- Client's interests and hobbies
- Exceptions to the problem

Think about what you have written and how the things you have written 'might' be helpful in moving forward (nothing is definite as the client agenda and journey may lead to different utilizations). What is important is that you are actively listening and, post-meeting, remembering what you heard that tells you that you are working 'with' the client and not 'on' the client.

KEY TERMS USED IN THIS CHAPTER

Problem-free talk, listening, openings, strengths, utilization, exceptions, alliance, praise, disclosure, SHUSH.

SUGGESTED FURTHER READING

Duncan, L., Ghul, R., & Mousley S. (2007). *Creating positive futures: solution focused recovery from mental distress.* London: BT Press.
The Solution Focused Measure of Occupational Function and the worksheets contained in this book will be familiar to many people working in the helping professions as they are not unlike many established, problem focused tools, yet on closer examination, they are poles apart and are truly inspirational in being able to 'see through' the problems without ignoring them. Rayya Ghul's opening chapter explains eloquently by asserting that people are functioning, unique individuals, in the way written about in this chapter.

4

PRE-SESSION CHANGE, EXCEPTIONS AND COPING QUESTIONS

LEARNING OUTCOMES

By the end of this chapter the reader will:

- Appreciate and understand what comes after openings in SFBT
- Understand what is meant by 'pre-session change' in SFBT and how to explore this
- Understand the meaning of and use of 'exception finding'
- Appreciate the use of coping questions in SFBT

PRE-SESSION CHANGE

It is useful to remember that days, weeks, or even months may have passed between the referral and the first meeting with the solution focused worker. Things change! So an exploration of any changes that have occurred between the client making a referral or having an assessment is useful for a number of reasons.

It sets the framework of fluidity; nothing is static. By this I mean that an enquiry into what has changed between referral and meeting gives the client the opportunity to think about any changes that have happened, and gives the therapist a chance to explore those changes. Changes may be full of examples of exceptions; they may be able to highlight efforts made by the client. One client I saw had recently received a diagnosis of a thyroid problem between referral to the mental health services and the time I first met him. He therefore realized that it was a physical condition that was making him lethargic and therefore depressed and down. This understanding meant that our work together was very different from how it might have been before he and I knew this. Had I have taken his referral on face value – 'Low in mood and with little motivation' (from his doctor) – without checking out any pre-session change I may well have had to backtrack somewhere during our first meeting. As it was, he was quite relieved to have a medical diagnosis and he wanted to focus on acceptance of that and 'looking after myself with this condition'.

Another client had decided, between making the referral and turning up for the first meeting, that he did not have a real investment in 'getting better' (initial referral information) as he had realized that with only two years to go until retirement age, 'getting better' meant returning to work, which he did not want. He wanted, instead, to focus on 'coping better' with the feelings he had. Again, had I not asked if anything had changed, some of the focus of the work may have been very different, with me assuming he wanted to improve and return to work as originally stated. This case is a good example of how people sometimes get an appointment to see the therapist and then start thinking about what they want and how therapy might be, before they arrive. We should never ignore or negate this process, and exploring pre-session change seems to be an ideal vehicle for this exploration.

This exploration of pre-session change not only determines a clearer direction for the work, it also allows the client and therapist to recognize any skills or resources that may have been utilized recently. So if the client has managed to reduce their drinking before coming to the meeting (even for that day), how come? What did they do that helped them? Who else may have helped them? And so on. It also shows interest in the client. The fact that you are not just interested in what it says on the referral form, but are also interested in finding out a bit more about how things have been, can only be good for building a therapeutic relationship, which is essential in any work of this kind.

It could be argued that to rely simply on referral and/or assessment information (though they have an important role of course) is not paying due heed to the client and their 'current' situation. One of the best referral letters I ever had was from a GP who wrote simply: 'Can you please see this young man. He is depressed for no apparent reason.' This was a source of amusement in the psychology department, with several therapists stating how outrageous it was that the doctor gave no history, no presenting circumstances, no patient observations, and so on. I pointed out to those therapists that having no prior information or knowledge meant that I had to start from scratch and find out from the client what they wanted out of the referral. This was great for me as a SF brief therapist.

Pre-session change can also highlight exceptions (to the problem) and 'exceptions' are explored in more depth later in this chapter. These exceptions or changes are the start of seeing where the therapist and client are heading. Not only does it help with focus, but pre-session change gives us the first real opportunity to amplify any positive changes. As stated, there is often weeks, sometimes months, between a client making a referral and coming to a first session. Often the situation that warranted the referral has changed a little, sometimes greatly.

CASE EXAMPLE: DEPRESSION AND LONELINESS

T: So Brian, it has been some weeks since you had an assessment here. Can you tell me, has anything changed at all since that time?

C: Well, I'm still depressed like, but when I first came I was on the dole, but now I've got a bit of work with me mate.

T: Great, how do you manage to get that?

C: Well, I bumped into him and he said did I want a day's work labouring, so I did, and then I asked him to give me a ring if he had anything else. He never rang me for a few days so I rang him, and he gave me another couple of days, and it's been pretty solid since then.

The client had pursued an offer of work between referral and first meeting, and stuck to task. Once I found out that he was working, it gave me and the client additional resources to explore. With a solution focused listening ear I had formulated some thoughts to ask questions. Such as:

Does working now mean you have a little more money? If so, what do you do with it? What does this mean for your goals of recovering from depression?

Now you are working, does that mean that you are around people [he had stated on his assessment information that he was quite lonely]?

The fact that he had 'bumped into' a mate told me that he had some friends at least, that he was reliable and/or skilled enough to be offered work. I went on to explore the positive impact that work was having on him and anything else of relevance before moving on to ask what he hoped to achieve from the session.

The point here is that I am formulating questions based around the client's functionality, not his dysfunction or 'problem'. Unfortunately, people in the helping professions are often trained to listen for 'triggers' as to what is making things go wrong. SF brief therapists are trained to listen for triggers as to what is going right or for what has helped things not to go wrong.

It is important to note here that I did not, at this early point in therapy, challenge the client's self-construction of being depressed. It would have achieved little other than to potentially alienate him. I call this 'ignoring' issues that other therapists from other models might focus on, 'benign neglect'. Instead, later on I asked how he would know when he is no longer depressed, what he would notice that is different? Again, a difference from problem focused or problem solving therapy is seen here. Rather than challenge the client and/or their self-identification of the problem, or themselves in relation to the problem, the SF brief therapist takes an 'observational' tack with the client, asking them to 'notice' what will be different when the problem is less or no longer there.

CASE EXAMPLE: OCD

T: Peter, it mentions on your [referral] form that up to six hours a day is taken up with your rituals and OCD behaviours. Is that still the case or has anything changed since your first assessment?

C: No, I mean, yes, it did change. It got much worse, but then it got a lot better.

T: Really? Can you tell me a bit more about that?

C: Well, it was like, everything I was doing was OCD. It was too much, even watching telly, I had to have the remote a certain way on the table, the volume set at an even number, odd numbers bother me. I couldn't eat anything without doing some things first. It got so bad I really thought about whether or not life was worth living any more.

T: That sounds really tough, a complete pain, your whole life being dominated by this. Is it still like that for you? You mentioned that it has got a lot better?

C: No, that's what I mean. It got so bad I had to do something about it so I have been making myself ignore some of the things sometimes.

T: And it's been better?

C: Yeah, better than when I saw the doctor even. I keep slipping a bit but most of the time it is less than before. At least I can watch a whole telly programme now or a film on the net.

T: How on earth did you manage to do that? What did you do? I mean, it must have been hard I guess?

From this conversation, I discovered that Peter had looked up OCD on the internet and had come across some 'self-help' exercises, which were CBT in nature, and they had been really helpful. He had also asked his parents (with whom he lived) to stop doing things for him to make things 'easier', such as putting his cereal into his breakfast bowl rather than watch him struggle to count the rice grains. By 'helping' him, they were in fact compounding the OCD as he did not have to challenge his behaviours or move on from them. He simply avoided them by allowing his parents to do things for him. So his pre-session change was that he had discovered some helpful things and it was my job to encourage him to do more of the same and to establish what his future goals were.

As mentioned earlier, the birth of the solution focused approach was a pragmatic one and many SF brief therapists still hold on to that principle. Peter found CBT techniques useful so I encouraged him to use more of them. Some became adapted to an SF slant. He had found an 'anxiety ladder' which encouraged him to 'score' how anxious he was if he did not do certain things, such as 'checking'. I adapted that into a ladder so that he could 'score' how calm he felt in certain situations where he did not do certain things. With this different slant we could work on what helped him to stay calm.

Like all of the cases I have included in this book, there are exceptions in pre-session change that are not so positive. I remember one young woman who told me that things had got so much worse that she did not know how she could go on. The therapist's role here is to establish what the client is doing to cope with this negative pre-session change, and what she was doing before that actively prevented things getting so bad previously. In this particular case, that avenue proved fruitless. On further exploration she expressed real suicidal intent and I had to refer the client to the emergency psychiatric team.

We must always take a deteriorating situation seriously in terms of risk. One of the criticisms sometimes levied at SFBT is that we overlook risk in favour of safety and positivity. This seems to be based on a misunderstanding of SFBT. Yes, we do have a positive outlook and we actively look for things that are helpful, but we must always remember that we have a duty and obligation (sometimes a legal obligation) to ensure that we do what we can when someone is unsafe and at risk.

There are also instances when either things have not changed significantly for clients or the client cannot relate any significant change to you. Sometimes this may just mean that they have not realized or noticed that things have changed. Sally was in this category.

SALLY

T: Can you tell me, Sally, has anything changed that you want to tell me about since your GP suggested you come here? Has anything got better or worse, even slightly?

[*Long pause.*]

S: No, I just exist. Days just turn into more days. It's all the same.

Now I could have chosen to challenge this and probe deeper. However, at our first meeting I sensed Sally's vulnerability and fragility so instead I chose to simply acknowledge that and move on. This is important. Do not press on with any SF intervention if it is not right and presents a risk of making things worse for the client and or the therapeutic relationship. Our primary role as therapists in any model is to do no harm. In Sally's case we looked more at how she coped with this level of 'existence', how she carried on.

EXCEPTIONS IN SFBT

About ten years ago, as part of our Project we learned that *exceptions* are at least important as the rules, if not more so. (de Shazer, 1994: 31)

Why are exceptions (to the problem) so important? Quite simply, exceptions show us and the client(s) that the 'problem' is not always there, or it is at least sometimes less of a problem. If the problem is not always there, then something else must be there instead... the 'not problem' or solution? Amplifying the times when the problem is not there and looking for patterns, behaviours and events that *are* present leads the solution focused brief therapist and client into looking for something different (George, Iveson & Ratner, 1999). When a client says 'I always feel depressed' or 'I can never say no to a drink', it is worth exploring further. Was there a time when the client wasn't depressed, or are there days when they were less depressed? Does the client ever say no to a drink? When did the client last say no to a drink? Determining these times, however small, gives us and the client a lead into more solution talk.

Some SF brief therapists have categorized exceptions into 'random' exceptions and 'deliberate' exceptions (Berg & Miller, 1992). Random exceptions are exceptions that just seem to occur, such as 'there was a day last week where things seemed better'. Our task then is to examine and explore that time in detail, paying attention to what the client noticed about that time. What was helping? Was the exception attributed to a time of day, a place, the company they were in, the weather, etc. We should then amplify the conditions noticed and/or see if there is a way of making those conditions, or part of those helpful conditions, occur again, turning the random exception into a deliberate one. It is always interesting to hear when someone simply attributes things being better to everything other than themselves or the actions they may have taken. Often they have been active participants in the exceptions without even realizing it. One client told me that she was extremely 'pissed off' that her vehicle had broken down and that she had needed to get into town. She walked the two miles there and two miles back and only realized when she got home that she had actually enjoyed the walk, which in turn had lifted her mood.

When an exception is 'deliberate' we again explore, in detail, what happened. We pay particular attention to what the client did to help this exception to occur and/or continue. Berg and Miller (1992: 107) show this in a client recollection: 'I just keep positive thinking. Whenever I pray it helps. Going to A.A. meetings helps. I've been really busy. When I feel productive, I don't need to drink.' If we find an exception (and we will), we should look at what was/is happening differently then. Did the client last feel less depressed when it was sunny? When they visited friends? Did the client last say no to a drink when they were driving? When they were with their family? Can the above situations be re-created? Are there strategies that can be employed where these exceptions might happen again? Look for reasons:

'So the last time you felt less depressed was when you were working. Is that because you were busy, or is there another reason that you felt a bit better?'

'When you knew you had to get up for an interview you drank less the night before and refused a drink. How did you manage that?'

Exceptions give us clues to:

- Differences: What is different about the exception? Is it place? Is it setting? Is it company? Is it that someone is utilizing skills?
- Skills: What skills were at play that helped the exception to happen? Was the client aware of those skills? Did the client use them deliberately?
- Resources: Who helped? What did the client have at hand that was helpful?

Exceptions also provide a healthy balance to how people (and therapists) view their situation (Wills, 2008). People tend to come to therapy with a focus on the problem and many forms of therapy, as mentioned previously, work on that focus. Exception-finding questions, leading to amplifications of those exceptions, allow both client and therapist to focus on a much more positive outlook.

SALLY

I asked about exceptions throughout the time I spent with Sally, in most meetings. The first meeting highlighted only one small exception, but later sessions highlighted more.

T: You mentioned, Sally, that things are pretty much the same, pretty much all of the time. Are there any exceptions to that, any times when things feel a little brighter?

S: No, not that I can think of.

T: When your mood lifts slightly, even for a second, or a minute?

S: No. Well, maybe. When I know my husband is not worrying about me it takes a bit of pressure off me, but I wouldn't say I feel brighter, no.

T: Would it be fair to say, though, and please tell me if I have got this wrong, that when you know Mick is not worrying, you feel a little 'better' [I shrugged my shoulders at this point to illustrate I was not sure].

S: Not 'better' but maybe not as bad.

T: And are there any other times when you don't feel 'as bad' that you can think of, at all?

S: Not right now.

I went on to talk to Sally in that first meeting about how I had noticed that she really cared about her husband, about her dog and about her family. She acknowledged this. While this was not saying to her directly that she had things to live for, she clearly viewed caring about and for others as important.

You will note that after her first 'denial' of any exceptions I asked Sally again, gently, with a little more detail. She then mentioned an exception and called it 'not as bad'. This gentle persistence is a useful technique to use with the caveat that if, after two or three questions there is still no positive response, move on. We should never be an 'interrogator'. We should, however, realize that the way we use language is not always understood or appreciated by the people we see. This is not patronizing; it is simply an acknowledgement that we are used to asking questions in a certain way. Clients are not often familiar with this and may need further clarification before they can answer effectively.

COPING QUESTIONS IN SFBT

Not everyone is ready all the time to move forward in a solution focused way (honestly!), or ready to be positive or to respond positively to a stranger in the therapy room asking endless questions. Someone may have huge and/or enduring problems, things can seem very hard, and they may not be 'ready' to engage fully with the process.

All the solution talk in the world may not change things (yet). We must remain 'solution focused' without becoming 'solution forced'. Remember the agenda, the goals and the pace belong to the client and we must always ensure that we hold on to that. If we force our agenda on people, if we force the pace, if we force them to answer questions when they are not ready or able to, we risk losing any therapeutic alliance and/or momentum we have established.

So, in these situations where people are not 'moving' along as we might like or expect, we assume at the very least that people are somehow coping to a degree, that they are managing on some level. The solution focused view is of capability, competence and functionality unless proved otherwise. Some coping and managing questions that we might ask are:

> 'I can see that is really hard, how do you manage to get through?'
> 'What has kept you going?'
> 'With all that going on how do you cope?'
> 'How do you manage to get by?'

There is also the use of observational statements that can highlight the therapist's view of competency and resilience. For example:

> 'With all that happening, you found the strength to get here today. I'm guessing that took some doing.'
> 'It is impressive that you have somehow managed to keep going.'

'Somehow' is a great word. I have seen it used frequently by de Shazer on videos. It is gentle and it assumes that clients are 'overcoming', at least in part.

Remember, if a client is sitting in front of you, they *are* coping. Maybe not as well as they would like, but they are coping. It may be because they have supportive family or friends, they may have a job that they like, or a hobby, and we need to elicit from them what gets them through. We can ask the miracle question at this point (see Chapter 6), or ask scaling questions (see Chapter 5) or look for ever smaller exceptions.

CASE EXAMPLE: BEREAVEMENT

T: Are there days when you cope better than other days?

C: Sometimes. It is not easier, it's just that I'm doing something and I forget, for a minute or two. Then I realize again that she's gone and I miss her all over again.

T: Of course. What's happening in those minutes that makes it easier to cope, even just for those few minutes?

(Continued)

(Continued)

C: Not sure, I know I should say to you it's because I'm busy, but most of the time even when I'm busy I can't stop myself thinking. I keep thinking I should, but I can't. I should do by now, shouldn't I?

T: Really, that is not for me to say. It is your loss, you deal with it in any way that is right for you. ... You mentioned that you wanted to be able to 'get on' without forgetting Julie. Sometimes, in 'getting on' or 'coping', it might be useful to notice what is 'getting on' a bit better, or 'coping' a bit better.

C: I suppose when I go to the grave and talk to her; that helps. I cry buckets, but when I get home I feel like I can get on a bit because I've seen her and talked to her. I don't go everyday anymore, just a couple of times a week. I suppose that shows I am coping a bit better.

What will the client notice that tells them (or others) that they are coping a little better? What will be even slightly different? This exploration of how people cope is always something I have seen utilized by experienced solution focused brief therapists, but is often forsaken by novices as they try to focus on being over-positive.

If a client feels they can't cope or can't see a way forward, what have they got that they can cling to? SFBT used to use the question 'What's happening that you want to continue to have happening?' (it is a bit of a mouthful). We could ask 'Are there things in your life that are stable – house, relationship, roof over your head, friends?' If a client can acknowledge that one thing is stable or OK or good, then other things can be too. We should highlight areas of stability and coping and explore what is helping. Can what is helping be applied to the more unstable or difficult parts of their life? If a client displays a complete lack of coping, then clearly the therapist has a role in alerting services that may be needed to keep them safe.

We recognize that people are resilient and resourceful, but often they do not realize that themselves. It is often comforting to people that the therapist points out the things that they have noticed (based wholly on client responses) that indicate to the client that they are somehow managing, often in spite of huge issues.

SALLY

I spent a lot of the time in the first few meetings with Sally simply acknowledging her lot and asking how she coped and managed with her situation as it was, often going over and over the same ground. To my recollection the following piece of narrative was from the third meeting.

T: We have talked a bit about the 11 months since the operation and the illness, and how hard it has been. How did you start to learn to manage afterwards, because it must have been a lot of changes to cope with in a short time?

S: Like I've said before, I'm not really managing, that's why my doctor wanted me to come here in the first place. I cry all the time, I miss everything I used to do, I want to work but I can't, I want to feel like there is some point to it all but there's not, and I'm gonna be like this for what, another 40 years?

T: I have no idea how bad that must feel, but I do have some idea, or at least can imagine how hard it must be to get through each day, doing the cleaning, cooking, looking out of the window, passing the hours waiting for Mick to come home. How do you manage that? How do you manage the boredom you talked about even? How do you cope at all?

S: I just do. It's not fair for Mick to see me down all the time, and he always asks me what I've managed to do in the day or what the day has been like, so I have to do something, like today I've come here, or I've got nothing to tell him: 'Hi Mick, I just sit here all day feeling shit, wishing I never woke up', so I have to just keep on, and on, and on [*starts crying again*].

T: And somehow you do. That really is quite something. You find something to do every day so you can talk to him about it.

S: At least he is there at weekends and he tries really hard to cheer me up. [*And here came the second small exception.*]

T: Does he ever succeed in that, in cheering you up, I mean?

S: A bit I suppose. Last week he took me to the seaside. I was upset that I couldn't walk on the beach. I was frightened of falling over and of going down the steps. I never used to be frightened of anything much, but we sat on a bench eating ice cream with his arm round me. It felt all right for a few minutes and it wasn't even that warm.

At this point I expressed some amazement and pleasure at this recollection, but probably overcooked it as Sally immediately retreated into problem talk again. The point, however, was not lost on me, and her as it transpired later. She actually had begun to appreciate, and even long for, these small moments of feeling 'all right'. It helped her cope in an otherwise difficult life.

RECAP: PRE-SESSION CHANGE, EXCEPTIONS AND COPING QUESTIONS

In this chapter you have read about the importance of recognizing that change can happen even before the therapy begins. You will also have noted that there are many ways to listen for and find exceptions, and that when found they should be explored, expanded on and amplified. Finally, you will have noted that SFBT is not always 'dynamic' in its movement. Sometimes noting how people cope and manage is addressed with more vigour than forward movement. You will also note that a lot of this chapter has talked about 'pace' and not going too quickly for the client. Brief does not always mean quick.

PERSONAL REFLECTION

Think about a time in your life when things were difficult. This does not have to be a life-changing event, but could be exam stress or an argument with a friend. How did you cope? What did you do that helped? Whose support did you seek? Even in those times, were there little glimmers of hope? Were there exceptions to the problem? For instance, when stressed out by work, what happened at weekends that meant the stress was relieved?

TRY THIS

If you have a colleague, acquaintance or friend who often has a certain way of being that you do not particularly like (maybe they are often rude, maybe they talk very loudly, maybe they are often pessimistic), play the detective (again) on the next three occasions you see them. Your mission is to notice any small (or large) exceptions to their behaviour. What happened when you noticed an exception? Was it a certain setting, place or time? Who was round, and how did it happen? Even if you cannot notice an exception, then you must notice how you and others around this person cope or manage this behaviour.

KEY TERMS USED IN THIS CHAPTER

Pre-session change, exceptions, coping, managing, pace.

SUGGESTED FURTHER READING

Berg, I. K., & Miller S. D. (1992). *Working with the problem drinker: a solution-focused approach.* New York: W. W. Norton.
This is a great book that has really useful case studies. I would particularly refer the reader to the explanation of the differences between random and deliberate exceptions (see pp. 108–110). Interestingly, Berg and Miller still use the categorization of relationship types into 'customer', 'complainant' and 'visitor relationships' (pp. 18–29). While this categorization has all but been dropped from the solution focused repertoire, mainly as practitioners started to categorize clients instead of relationships, it is still useful to read about it and I still pay some heed to it, at least in my thought processes.

Burns, K. (2005). *Focus on solutions: a health professional's guide.* London: Whurr Publishers.
Kidge Burns has a really nice way of illustrating the use of coping questions (see pp. 26–28 and 78–81 in particular).

5

THE USE OF SCALES IN SFBT

LEARNING OUTCOMES

By the end of this chapter the reader will:

- Appreciate the use of scaling in SFBT
- Understand how scaling is used in relation to other interventions, such as the miracle question, and as a unique intervention
- Appreciate that scaling can be used at almost any point of an SF conversation

SCALING

A characteristic technique of SFBT, and one that is used by other models, is scaling. It is used at almost any point in a solution focused conversation. This chapter could have come almost anywhere in this book for that reason alone. It is useful to examine the use of scales in their own right, as well as their role within SFBT practice specifically.

Often multiple scale questions are used in a session. This is another reason why it is useful to take notes in sessions. Scales seem to come quite easily to most therapists and most clients. We use them in SFBT in the following ways:

- To validate clients' experiences and descriptions of their situation in the past, present and future
- To serve as a benchmark of progression towards the client's preferred future
- To act as a tool of shared meaning
- To act as a goal-oriented part of our conversations

- To be an observational and comparative tool
- To measure confidence
- To measure the likelihood of something happening, such as task completion

A normal scale is from 0 to 10, though if a client has their own version, such as 0–100, then use it. Often clients do not start off by using scales. Rather, they say things like 'I feel much better'. It may therefore be useful to get them to gauge that by using a scale to see how much better, say 10%?

Children often use their own version of scales and we need to be creative and enquiring when working with younger children to establish exactly what they mean when they talk in degrees or scales. A good example of this is a teenager I once worked with. We shared with amusement a scaling interpretation of their displeasure in coming to see me. It went something like this:

> Refusal to speak was equivalent to 10 out of 10 in terms of displeasure
> 'I fucking hate coming here' was equivalent to 9 out of 10 in terms of displeasure
> Right down to 'I don't care' being 2 out of 10 on the displeasure scale and 'If you want' or 'I s'pose' (I suppose) being 1 out of 10.

We then turned this on its head and made 'I s'pose', 10 out of 10 of being OK at being in the session. This use of shared meaning let the client know that I was aware that they were mostly there under sufferance. Once this was out of the way we could get on with some work.

It is important to remember that the use of scales is not an alien concept, although putting numbers to words is sometimes new to us. We actually use scales all the time, for example:

> I have no appetite at all = 0?
> I am not hungry = 1?
> I'm not that hungry = 2
> I feel a bit peckish = 3–4?
> I am getting hungry = 5–6?
> I am pretty ravenous now = 7?
> I could eat a horse = 8?
> I'm starving = 9?
> If I don't eat something soon I'm going to pass out = 10?

Take a moment to think about all the other things that we 'scale' in different ways on a regular basis: anger, energy levels, happiness, etc.

Wherever someone puts themselves on the scale, remember, it is their scale. It is vital to establish what that means to them, and why? If someone states that they are 1, 2 or 3 out of 10 (the number is less relevant than the explanation), we ask something about that generally in a positive framework:

> T: OK, so you have put yourself at 1 out of 10, when 0 out of 10 is the worst that your drinking has been, and 7 out of 10 is the day that you know things

have begun to get better for you, the 'wonderful' day. What puts you at a 1 today? What has moved you up from 0?

C: Well, I came here, so that's a start. I am doing something and I've not had a drink yet today.

[*From here we can explore the 'hows', and use the response to amplify the client's achievements thus far.*]

T: Wow, so you have managed to resist a drink today and started to get some help. Sounds like you are serious …. I wonder, what will you notice that tells you (and others) that you have reached a 2 out of 10, not got to that 7 out of 10, but just a little further towards it?

C: Mmmm, I suppose if I go without a drink for a whole day, or at least until the evening.

[*NB: The client has articulated in the negative (many do). The absence of the problem is only a part of the goal; it is our job to find out what they will be doing instead.*]

T: So going without a drink would move you up your scale. What do you think the benefits of not drinking all day might be for you? What might be different on that day?

C: I'll be able to get things done, plus I'll have a bit more money, and I won't be so hung-over tomorrow.

T: What will you be able to get done? [*ignoring the 'not hung-over' part of the reply.*]

C: Well, I can go down to the benefits office and get all that sorted. I could start looking at jobs as well, I suppose. I need to see my folks too 'cause my mum is not so well.

T: Gosh, so at 2 out of 10, you will really start to do more stuff. Will your mum notice anything different when you go to see her?

C: She'd be pleased, so yeah, she would see that I'm getting my shit together.

So small questions about scales can lead to much more: an exploration of client goals, a systemic view of how others will benefit from an improvement and, most importantly of all in my opinion, a renewed optimism.

There are a few clients who scale themselves as 0 out of 10. If they do, you need to consider if non-therapeutic interventions are needed for the client's safety. However, does 0/10 necessarily mean total despair? Why not ask, remembering the coping questions of the last chapter: 'How on earth do you keep going?' Or 'How do you cope when you are feeling so low?' For example, when asked, a 0 out of 10 client once said: 'If it wasn't for my kids I'd kill myself'. We looked further into what being a mum meant to her, and how she coped with all the things a mum has to do, even when feeling so down about her drinking. She actually told me tremendous things about how she managed as a parent on a relatively low income, how she never drank in front of her children, and so on. I ignored her alcohol problem (skilful neglect) and spent the rest of the session talking to her about her parenting skills, and we agreed a between-session task based on that. At the next session her drinking had reduced considerably in direct relation to more time spent with her children. This is also an example of the solution not being tied to the problem.

Sometimes 0 out of 10 is the client's way of letting you know just how bad things are. We should respect this and not negate it. What we do need to do is establish what this 0 out of 10 looks like and what 1 out of 10 or 2 out of 10 might look like. To ask a client 'how' they will get to the next point on the scale is a behaviouralist intervention. To ask what it will 'look like' or how they will know they are there is more of an observational or interactional intervention. It also assumes that this is going to happen.

I once had a client who scaled themselves at −99 out of 10. On further exploration, something told me to ask *'How come not −100?'* She replied, 'That would be suicidal, I'm not quite there yet.' When that particular client said at their closing session that they were 0 out of 10, it was a sure sign that things were on the up and that they had achieved their goal of 'Coming to terms with the shit I've been through in the last year'. I have to say, explaining to my supervisor that someone had a planned discharge and had reached her goals at 0 out of 10 made for an interesting conversation.

CONFIDENCE SCALES

Having confidence in achieving a goal, in getting better, in overcoming something is very important. Scaling can be a really useful tool in achieving this, not just to measure that confidence, but also to look at how a level of confidence (regardless of where on the scale) is understood by the client and therapist and what might be happening when that confidence is higher.

CASE EXAMPLE: ANXIETY

T: So, going to Leeds on the bus is something that will tell you that you have managed your anxiety better. You have told me that you are planning to do this next Monday, a brave step, and scary [*client nods*]. How confident on a scale of 0 to 10, where 10 means nothing can stop you and 0 is that it is just a dream that won't happen, are you?

C: Probably about 7.

T: How come? What puts you at 7?

C: I'm determined, and I went to the bus station and got a timetable. I know how long it takes and where to get off, and if the bus is late, there is one every 20 minutes so it isn't too long to wait.

T: You seem to have covered a lot there. I wonder if, somehow, your confidence changed to an 8 out of 10, how would you know? What would be different?

C: I'd be less worried about freaking out on the bus. I don't think I will 'coz I'm taking my headphones and a magazine, you know that distraction thingy we talked about before.

> T: OK, so what does 8 out of 10 look like? What would give you just that little bit more confidence, do you think?
>
> C: Erm, buy two magazines in case I have to read through the first one.
>
> Both I and the client laughed at this. The client did in fact buy two magazines but did not need to read either.

Another use of a confidence scale that has proved useful is to relate it to time. I discovered this by accident and with the help of a client. I asked a client how confident they were that they would be able to get back to work. They were on long-term sick leave at the time after a bullying incident. They told me that they would be able to get back to work when they had time to recover and feel strong again.

> ## CASE EXAMPLE: OFF WORK DUE TO BULLYING
>
> T: So when some time has passed and you feel strong again, you want to go back to work. Have I got that right?
>
> C: Yeh, not yet though. I still feel pretty raw and I can't face people in the office yet.
>
> T: On that scale I mentioned where 10 out of 10 means you will definitely feel confident enough to return to work at some point, where are you, in terms of confidence?
>
> C: What, now?
>
> T: Yes, right now, on a scale out of 10 of *ever* being able to go back to that job.
>
> C: Oh, I'll go back, 10 out of 10. I won't let them beat me, I just have to get stronger.
>
> T: So you are 10 out of 10 confident of going back at some point. How confident are you of being back in say, a year?
>
> C: 10.
>
> T: Oh, OK. Say six months?
>
> C: 10.
>
> T: Three months?
>
> C: About 6 I think.
>
> T: Right, so, tell me if I have got this wrong. You feel that between three and six months is how long it will take you, with some degree of confidence to get back to work?
>
> We went on to establish that she felt she was getting stronger all the time and that her levels of confidence were directly related to this fact. She was healing in her own time. In fact, she returned sooner than she had suggested and we closed our work together a month after she had returned.

I have since combined time and confidence in a scale on a number of occasions and it has proved useful for the most part. This is a good illustration of something I never learned from a book (though of course the reader of this book may do now) but directly from following the client's lead. Indeed, many of the best interventions that I have made have been as a direct result of learning from clients, not from books or other colleagues.

As well as confidence scales I sometimes use *likelihood scales*. I might ask something like: 'On a scale of 0 to 10, where 0 represents no chance at all and 10 represents "absolutely definitely", how likely is it that you will get better/achieve your task, etc.?' This is slightly different from a confidence scale in that it allows a client to move away from their own construct of their confidence and move into possibilities. For example, someone once told me that they were not that confident of being happy but that they knew most people 'got over' depression. In other words, it was 'likely'.

SALLY AND SCALING

At Sally's first meeting we never really established a firm goal other than her GP wanting her to feel better. However, I did ask her where she thought, on a scale of 0 to 10, 'feeling better' might be. Her response led to a greater examination of scales:

S: Feeling better? I can't feel better if I can't get better (physically), that's the point.

T: Sorry. OK, that was a bit clumsy of me. So if, say, there is a 0 to 10 scale of how you feel, where 10 is the best you could imagine feeling, given your situation, 10 is where your doctor thinks you have got better, and in your head, even though you are not physically any better, you do feel better, where on that scale are you now?

[Sally did not answer, for what seemed an awfully long time.]

S: I don't know, 0 out of 10. I don't see the point of this question. My GP wants me to feel better, but he doesn't really get it. There isn't any hope of that for me. I know he wants me to feel better, so does Mick, everyone does.

T: OK, I can see this is hard, and I don't want to upset you more than you are. Can I just ask one more question about maybe what Mick would see that tells him that maybe you have moved off that 0 out of 10?

S: He already thinks I am getting better because I keep the house OK and cook for us and go out when he wants us to, and I go to the doctors, and I'm coming here. He doesn't know that inside I am at 0.

T: Mmmm, so, if inside, you moved off the 0, to, I dunno, maybe .5, what would *you* notice that told you this, or Mick, or the GP, or me? We might not notice, but you might.

S: That's, well, I can't really think. All I can think is that I'd be feeling better. I feel like we are going round in circles here.

T: I'm sorry, it doesn't sound like I am being very useful for you at the moment. Maybe I am rushing you.

S: No, it's not that. It's just I can't think past this, what I'm doing everyday, how I'm feeling. Maybe something will get me interested in something and make me feel a bit better, I dunno.

I went on in that session to keep validating Sally's experiences, and did not pursue the scaling questions any more, although in the end-of-session feedback I reflected back to her that she had arrested the decline and was coping. I also pointed out to her that she had said 'maybe' something would get her interested. This is important: she had said 'maybe'. She was open to the possibility that things could get better even though her statements did not reflect this. It is also useful to note that others thought she was probably higher than 0 out of 10. I could and probably should have explored this a bit further and have certainly heard other therapists do this, and I have done so myself with other clients. I could have asked 'So what does Mick see that tells him you are higher than 0 out of 10?'

Sally's between-session task (which she could not come up with and I had to suggest) was to notice any time at all between the first and second session when she had moved off 0 out of 10, even momentarily. She did not notice after this session but after a subsequent session, with the same task as she had wanted to continue with it, she did notice and feedback to me that her husband had paid for her to go to a hot spa and have a therapeutic massage. There was classical music playing in the background and she said 'just for a moment' things felt OK, maybe even as high as 5 out of 10. This was extremely significant and gave me a great inroad for the start of that session. This was probably a turning point in our work and while it had come about from the use of scaling, it is worth noting that Sally kept on with the same task for several sessions as it was proving helpful.

RECAP: THE USE OF SCALES IN SFBT

In this chapter you have read that the use of scales underpins much of Solution Focused Brief Therapy and that scales are utilized throughout the work. Scales are used alone or in conjunction with other interventions, such as the miracle question.

PERSONAL REFLECTION

Think about somewhere you want to be or something you want to achieve in your life. On a scale of 0–10, where 10 represents you being there or having achieved it and 0 represents you having made no movement at all towards it, where are you right now? What will one point up on that scale look like to you? What will it look like to others? What has got you to the point on the scale where you are now? How come? What else?

TRY THIS

With the very next client you see, whether they are an exiting client or one you have seen before, ask them this question: In relation to the goal you have set where 10/10 represents you having got there, where on that scale would you put yourself today? Wherever they place themselves on the scale, ask them how they might know if they have moved up slightly on the scale.

KEY TERMS USED IN THIS CHAPTER

Scales, scaling, confidence, likelihood, noticing.

SUGGESTED FURTHER READING

De Jong, P., & Berg, I. K. (2002). *Interviewing for solutions* (2nd Edn.). Belmont, CA: Brooks–Cole.
Although this interactional book is ideally read in conjunction with the video that accompanies it, it stands alone well in describing the use of scales in many different parts of the solution focused meeting. It is also a really good read, and an essential volume for the SF brief therapist's bookshelf.

Nelson, T. S. (Ed.) (2010). *Doing something different: solution-focused brief therapy practice*. New York: Routledge.
The first chapter in this edited volume by Coert Visser is a fantastic and brief example of scaling. Chapter 5 by Lee Shilts provides good examples of using scaling with couples, and Coert again talks of scales in Chapter 15 with a useful tool we can all use.

6

CO-CREATING PREFERRED FUTURES

LEARNING OUTCOMES

By the end of this chapter the reader will:

- Understand the use of the 'miracle question': how to ask it, when to ask it and why it is utilized
- Understand what is meant by a 'preferred future' in SFBT and how it becomes a focus of the work
- Appreciate the use of scaling in preferred futures and how it is used in relation to the miracle question and as a unique intervention

The previous chapter on scaling stands alone. However, scaling is inextricably linked to the miracle question in the model that is SFBT. Scaling can be used without the miracle question, though to use the miracle question without looking at a preferred future or using scaling does not seem possible, or if it is, it is certainly unusual.

THE WONDERFUL (MIRACLE) QUESTION

Most people who participate in SFBT training remember the 'miracle' question. Equally, most people get it somewhat wrong. They use it too quickly, or use bits of it, and often gallop through the responses that a client gives.

I will acknowledge from the outset that to use the miracle question well takes a great deal of skill in timing, listening, amplifying and exploration. To be clear, we use the miracle question:

- *To imagine what the future might look like.* This 'imagining' has some roots in hypnotherapy and visualization, of that there is little doubt. However, it is also a practical and cognitive application in that it allows the client to 'see' what the stages along the way of things being better might be.
- *To fix a clear goal(s).* Being clear about where they want to be or what they want to achieve is essential in that without this clarity we, and the client, risk ambiguous statements and goals such as 'I want to be better', 'I want to be normal'. This does not allow us either to use a clear scale point as a measure of progress, or work towards something concrete.
- *To create a future memory.* When we drive to a place we have been before we recognize 'landmarks'. The miracle question does exactly this. It gives the client 'landmarks' to recognize when they are on the way to their preferred futures.
- *To lead into scaling.* I have talked about scaling in the previous chapter. The miracle question is an excellent lead into using scales if you have not done so already in the session.
- *To narrow the intervention to a more solution oriented one.* When we use the miracle question we start to see where the client wants to be and what they want to achieve. Once we have the bare bones of a solution we can narrow the focus on to that solution and at the same time broaden the description of the narrow focus. If I ask someone what they want and they say 'to be happy' this is broad. I can narrow it by asking what they want to be happy with. Say their answer is that they want to be happy with their choice of place to live I can then broaden this by getting them to describe what that place looks like, and so on.
- *To allow the client to be 'descriptive'.* By narrowing the focus we have something we can concentrate on. At this point the miracle question helps us to allow the client to become very descriptive of how things might look beyond the problem, when the miracle has happened. It is extremely important, as will be seen later, to paint a picture in the mind of the 'miracle' day or time.
- *To bring significant others in to the picture.* Here we are back to the systemic idea that a client is not an island and that their miracle will be noticed by and have an impact on others – family, loved ones, friends, colleagues.

In short, the miracle question (MQ) allows us and the client to look for what will be different, and what differences might be apparent to them and others.

Many practitioners of SFBT would insist on using the miracle question in the first meeting with the client as this is enshrined in the EBTA research definition (see www.ebta.nu/sfbt-researchdefinition.pdf) and normal SFBT practice. For me, this is not essential, mainly because the first session may be taken up with all the things I have talked about thus far. Just as importantly, by insisting that the miracle question is utilized in the first session, we are at risk of setting the agenda and of making the clients fit the therapy, rather than the other way around.

Sometimes people want to spend the first session telling us how bad things have been, or at the very least giving us their history (of the problem). This is what most people expect to do when they go to see a therapist or counsellor. It is our job to listen to the client, not force our interventions on them too soon. However, we have to know when to intervene. By this I mean that there is a difference between simply using an intervention and utilizing the skills needed to know when to use that intervention. The miracle/wonderful question is a good intervention to help change 'problem talk' into 'solution talk'.

I have always been uncomfortable with the word 'miracle' – whether it was my early experiences of Catholicism that contributed to this, I'm not sure. However, I am sure that for some people the word 'miracle' does not fit. Do we risk offending a Muslim, for whom only Allah can make miracles happen, or a Buddhist, who does not believe in miracles? What about a lapsed Catholic? Or even more simply, does a 'miracle' imply some kind of divine intervention, something that the client cannot control? Personally, then, I very rarely use the word 'miracle'; I feel it is too culture-laden. I prefer to say 'something wonderful' – it just seems more in keeping with the real world too. This does not mean that I never use the word 'miracle' or that I judge others for using it, it is just a personal preference.

So, what exactly is the miracle/wonderful question and how is it asked? The first use of the miracle question is attributed to Insoo Kim Berg (de Shazer et al., 2007) but it is constantly being refined and asked differently. The definitive wording outlined by De Jong and Berg (1998: 77–8), is this:

> I want to ask you a strange question. Suppose that while you are sleeping tonight and the entire house is quiet, a miracle happens. The miracle is that the problem which brought you here is solved. However, because you are sleeping, you don't know that the miracle has happened. So you wake up tomorrow morning, what will be different that will tell you a miracle has happened and the problem which brought you here is solved?

This is but one version. I have seen many tapes of SF brief therapists and practitioners, including de Shazer and Berg. Not only did they rarely ask the question using exactly the same words each time, they also put different emphasis on different parts of the question, pausing in different places. This is something which comes with experience and confidence. Some practitioners who are new to SFBT find the question hard to ask and can be wary of the answers. It is worth persevering with it and I would direct you to Harry Korman's website (www.sikt.nu/engindex.html) where he gives an excellent rationale of why he still uses the question after two decades of being a SF brief therapist.

While the miracle question (in this format) is attributed to Berg in the context of SFBT, Coert Visser also acknowledges Eriksonian roots (see his website at http://solutionfocusedchange.blogspot.com/2007/10/who-invented-miracle-question.html). We should also recognize that Alfred Adler used a very similar set of words back in the 1920s and 1930s: 'If I had a magic wand or pill that would eliminate your symptoms immediately, what would be different in your life?' (Corsini, Wedding & Dumont, 2008: 65). This emphasis on difference – when the problem is receding or is no longer there at all – is something that is very prominent in SFBT.

The miracle question was originally intended as a prompt to a client imagining a life where the problem has gone. It supposes that things are going to get better. There are two main ways that practitioners ask the miracle question these days: sometimes they 'qualify' it, and sometimes they do not. Knowing when to qualify the miracle question and when not to do so is something that I and others have developed and honed over the years. I am not going to say that one way of asking the question is better than the other, I'll simply acknowledge the difference.

To explain further, one could ask the miracle question without qualifying by saying at the end, as described above, 'and your problem is solved' or 'and the problems you brought here today have disappeared', or a similar form of words. This is how the Milwaukee team and BRIEF generally have asked the question. This assumes a life post-problem that is quite different and can be extremely liberating. Although the use of the question in this way can, on occasion, be 'too broad' or too great a leap for some people (including the novice therapist), it is OK if the therapist feels confident in working with that, and many do.

The first few times I asked the miracle question I found it very challenging, not least because the first client I saw answered that he wanted his grandma to still be alive. This response was not at all what I was expecting as we were working with his heroin addiction. In truth, I was stumped and made a complete mess of the next few minutes. I had not qualified the miracle question to the issue at hand. If I got that answer now, I would acknowledge that this was his 10 out of 10, and that it couldn't happen, and that we needed to work on what could happen. I might even ask what difference his grandma being alive would make, and focus on anything that could still be there even though his grandma was not going to come to life. Based on the original wording of the miracle question, it is quite difficult and challenging to get it right, especially for the novice SF brief therapist. This is one of the reasons I tend to ask, and teach, the miracle question as a 'qualified' question. For example:

> 'And when you wake up, have you started to believe that you CAN stop drinking. What is the first thing that you notice that tells you?'
> 'And when you wake up, you realize that the depression is going to get better. What is the first thing you notice that tells you?'

An example of the question asked with a qualifier is as follows:

> 'I'd like to ask you another question. This one will take a bit of thinking about, a bit of imagination. Let's say that when you leave here today, you go home, do whatever you normally do and at some point go to bed and go to sleep. When you are asleep, something wonderful happens. That confidence that you talked about wanting somehow starts to be there. You do not know this has happened of course because you are asleep, but when you wake up, you realize that something wonderful has indeed happened and this confidence has started to be there. … How would you know this? What is the first thing that you would notice that tells you?'

The difference between the two approaches is clear. In the first approach a client may answer with anything. The answer may not even be related to the issue at hand: 'I would have won the lottery'. This is no bad thing as this might be their 10 out of 10; we are not there to judge, but to find out what the 'good enough' point on the scale might be.

The second approach is more defined and can be very specific. De Shazer asks a young man in a wheelchair a brilliant miracle question in his training video *I want to want to* (even though the video is a re-enactment). Before asking the full miracle question he qualifies the question by saying 'given your situation'. It is therefore a realistic question – the young man will not walk again. De Shazer is validating that reality, by asking what *CAN* happen. I certainly prefer to 'qualify' my miracle questions and sometimes in very small ways:

> 'So when you wake up, you haven't stopped taking heroin, you haven't even reduced, but somehow you know, you just know that this time things are going to be different. What do you think the first clue to that might be? How would you know?'

I have mentioned that I prefer the term 'something wonderful' rather than the word 'miracle' and I generally use this. I have, however, used the word 'miracle' when it fits (see below). I am not phobic about the word 'miracle'; I'm just uncomfortable with it:

> *T:* I want you to imagine that when you go to sleep tonight something wonderful happens and all the problems that you brought here today are gone when you wake up, you didn't … [*client interrupts*].
> *C:* That would be a miracle.
> *T:* Have you heard this question before?

[*Client and therapist laugh.*]

> *C:* No, why?
> *T:* OK, a miracle happens and …

Clients can be quite surprised at the miracle question and often answer in the negative: 'I won't be rattling' (a colloquial term for withdrawing from substances). A solution focused reflection might be: 'So if you are not rattling, what are you doing? How are you feeling instead?' 'I won't be feeling like I want the world to end' could elicit a solution focused response of 'How would you be feeling instead?' De Jong and Berg (2002) describe this 'looking for the instead' (not just in the miracle question) as 'the presence of some desirable behaviours rather than the absence of problems'.

I find it interesting that De Jong and Berg use the term 'behaviors' as I would personally describe it as the presence of desirable *situations* rather than the absence of problems. De Jong and Berg's term (2002) is more behaviouralist than observational, but the point made is similar: we are looking for what *will* be happening, not what will *not*.

From this point the therapist must look for the minutiae: 'What would you eat for breakfast? What would you be doing on that day? Who with?' etc. This is also an opportunity to focus on others: 'So would anyone else notice a difference? What would they notice? What would they say?'

The wonderful question is followed by time spent eliciting from the client what a day, week or month may look like when the 'problem' is gone. What would be different? Who would notice? etc. The miracle is like a stone thrown into a pool, with the ripples travelling across the water. The man who stops his problem drinking may have more money in his pocket to pay the bills, he may be able to spend more time with his children, be a better husband, be off work less, and so on. I like to spend a considerable time 'visualizing' with the client what might be different on this day and often end the day with a question like: 'So to bring you to the end of that day, you are lying in bed, dozing off, what do you think your last thoughts might be?' This is a great intervention as it leads the client into thinking not only about the day after the miracle, but the day after that, and even further into the future.

The wonderful question also presents an opportunity for the client to 'see' a future memory. Think of when we go shopping. We know where the cash point is, we can visualize the products and where they are in the store, and the journey home. We can even remember where we are going to put the produce, which shelves, etc. when we have returned home, even though we have not yet embarked on the journey.

The practitioner, in my opinion will gain maximum benefit for the client by taking time over this. Two minutes is not enough. I have spent a whole session getting people to visualize the day when things start to get better. It can be likened to a journey by car: we know where we start from, and we know where we want to end up, and we must notice along the way that we are on the right road to get there. This examination of the minutiae makes the day after the miracle/wonderful thing seem much more real, much more tangible, especially if the therapist can relate back, at each point, to the client what they are saying, and help them with this visualization. I am sure that I have been influenced by some of Erikson's writings here, or at least by those who wrote about him, though I doubt I will ever be a hypnotherapist – I prefer to 'tap into' the conscious visualizations of people.

I mentioned in an earlier book the 'poached egg man' (Hanton, 2003). This is a good illustration of how we can use minute details to recognize when a miracle has happened. My client was constantly hung-over, drank daily and in response to the miracle questioned replied that the first thing he would notice would be that he could eat breakfast. On further exploration he mentioned that he would love to sit down to a plate of poached eggs on toast as he had enjoyed this many years previously. We went through the stages of this happening: from him getting out of bed, having a shower, getting dressed, putting the toast in the toaster, putting the eggs on, where he would be sitting, what he could see in the room, whether he used salt, and so on. When he told me that he had indeed stopped drinking and had poached eggs on toast he related to me that he had said to his partner, at the breakfast table, that the miracle had happened. He used somewhat colourful language at this point.

A further example that illustrates the 'power' of looking for the minutiae is when I asked a colleague (not in a therapy session) the miracle question. She said she was fed up of getting home tired and just slumping in front of the TV. I asked her:

Me: Supposing tomorrow was different. You woke up, came to work and got home, something wonderful had happened and you were energized, you did not sit in front of the TV. What WOULD happen?

[The following words are not an exact replication as stated, but near enough.]

Colleague: Oh, I'd sort the garden out.
Me: OK, run me through that. You get home, how do you get to the garden?
Colleague: Through the kitchen.
Me: Explain to me, where is the door in relation to the kitchen? What do you have to do before going into the garden, if anything?
Colleague: The door leads from the kitchen directly into the garden, I have to put my boots on first.

Me:	Where are your boots? What colour are they? Why do you need your boots on first?
Colleague:	By the door, green, proper wellies [Wellington boots]. I need them on so I don't get my shoes muddy and bring the mud back into the house.
Me:	Oh, OK, you're going to get muddy then?
Colleague:	Yes, I need to walk across the grass, get all the rubbish, leaves, twigs, weeds, etc. sorted out. I haven't done much over winter at all, so it needs a good seeing to.
Me:	Do you need any tools?
Colleague:	Yes, I'd go to the shed and get the rake, maybe the pruning shears, a brush, a bag to put the rubbish in.
Me:	Yep, I can see all that, makes sense … so, supposing you did this for a while, and cleared some of the garden, what would that feel like? Would you feel any better?
Colleague:	Definitely [*laughs*] 8 out of 10. [*she is familiar with SFBT*]
Me:	And how do you feel on a night now, not doing this?
Colleague:	4 or 5.

She reported back to me at our next meeting that visualizing going into the garden, getting the tools, preparing for the task in hand was all very powerful for her. When she had gone home that day, she walked into the kitchen, saw the boots by the door and got out into the garden for two hours and felt invigorated.

Sometimes a client will answer the miracle/wonderful question with 'I don't know'. Not only should the therapist not be put off by this, we should be almost pleased to get this answer to what is a strange and often unexpected question. It is an entirely appropriate response (de Shazer, 1994). At this point, silence is golden. Wait a while, count to 10 in your head. More often than not the client just needs some thinking time to come up with something. If they do not respond, be gentle, acknowledge the difficulty of the question, probe a little more, based on the original way you asked the question:

> 'Mmm, I can see that is quite hard for you to answer … So, you wake up, and you notice a small thing, something different that tells you this miracle has happened, or started to happen. I wonder what that might be?'

If after this you still get no response, or a negative response, you could try broadening the question out:

> 'Even if you did not notice, do you think anyone else would notice a difference? Who maybe? What might they notice?'

The question is also a good opportunity to use scales. Is the day after the miracle a 10 out of 10 or an 8 out of 10? Where is the client now? What will the person notice that tells them that they have moved up the scale? How much distance (in scale points) is there between now and the day after the miracle?

Some SF practitioners always get the client to scale the day after the 'wonderful' as a 10 out of 10, assuming that the miracle/wonderful thing is the 10 out of 10. Personally, I feel this is an assumption too far and is therapist-led. Therefore, I prefer to get the person to scale it themselves by asking at the end of the narrative something like:

'So if 10 out of 10 represents the best that a day/your life could possibly be and 0 out of 10 represents the opposite, where would you put the day you have just described on a scale out of 10?'

From there we can ask where the client is today – we have a start point to the journey, an end point, and where people are now on that journey. Often, by asking the miracle question, then relating it to a before and after scaling question, the journey does not seem so arduous, and this is why I put these two interventions together in this chapter. Let me give you an example.

A particular asking of the miracle question led to a client stating that they would be 9 out of 10 on the scale if they felt happier and had gone out and met people socially instead of letting them down at the last moment. When asked where they were at that day, they reported 4 out of 10 on the same scale. This was because they were going to work and talking to people and they were coming for help. The space between 4 and 9 is only five points so we have established that some things are already happening to place someone on the scale. They have already started the journey. We have also established where on that same scale the end of that journey is. We have therefore started the work already and established the scope of what still needs to be done.

PREFERRED FUTURES

The miracle/wonderful question is central to SFBT, both in its original development as a model and in its continued use as an indicator that the therapeutic input is solution focused. What we are looking for by asking the miracle/wonderful question is a description of a preferred future. Generally, of course, for the client this means a future without the problem, or where the problem is less of a problem. What we are trying to establish and what we mean by a 'preferred future' in fact is something else entirely. It is that something will be happening instead of the problem, it won't be defined by the problem, but will be altogether different from the problem. This is one of the paradigm shifts in SFBT that is often talked about. The preferred future does not have to be tied inextricably to the problem present or past; it can (and should) be something else.

A future where someone is no longer using heroin is a future that is defined by the heroin problem. A future where someone is eating well is a future defined by the eating problem. A future defined by having more confidence is defined by having a lack of confidence previously. Our job is to help people imagine a future where they may be doing something they want to do – going to college, having a hobby, socializing, having a job, looking after their house.

Again, this preferred future does not 'have to' be determined by a problem past. I once worked with a young woman who had been living with anorexia and was now on a social work course. She told me: 'I want to be known as Becky the social worker, not Becky the recovering anorexic'. I could not have summed up the focus of SFBT better had I tried. This is another example of learning from a client – they are our best teachers.

I cannot state clearly enough how important this definition of 'something else' (other than the problem construct) is to SFBT. The miracle question and future scale points lead a client *to* where they want to be, not away from where they do not want to be. This shift in thinking is essential to SFBT. It defines the approach.

There are two important points to note in terms of looking at preferred futures with clients. First, in our work we may not reach the preferred future. We may only be part of the way there when a client and therapist stop working. This 'good enough' point is where the client, quite rightly, is on the road to that preferred future and takes over, wholly, that process for themselves. For example, a client once told me that she wanted a degree. This was when she actually had not been in any formal education or employment for a decade. The degree was her 10 out of 10. We stopped working together when she had started the course, some five months after we had started working together. She had gained confidence, been for interviews, been accepted on the course and was five or six weeks in. She told me that she was at 6 out of 10, but was confident it was going to be alright now.

The second note of importance is that preferred futures can change as people move towards them. Somebody wanting to have a wide circle of friends because they felt lonely told me later that the two friendships she had formed had made her realize that a 'wide' circle of friends was not necessary at all. The point here is to keep focus, keep checking in and do not assume that you, as the therapist, still know where you are going – not without the client's guidance anyway.

SALLY

I tried to ask the miracle question with Sally on two occasions: at our first meeting where it failed miserably, probably due to my bad timing, and again a few sessions in when Sally actually told me that the question was not relevant as she was not ready for miracles and wanted to carry on working as we were. We did, however, establish a preferred future quite early on which was that she wanted to be able to get on with her life without crying all the time or thinking about the operation and her life before it. These were quite negative goals determined and defined by the 'problem'. Making this a solution focused goal she decided that she wanted a future where she could 'at least have an interest in living'. I found this an eloquent and moving goal.

Later on, Sally's preferred future changed on several occasions from 'accepting how she was' to 'getting on with things' to more positive thoughts which I will come on to later. What was very interesting for me while working with Sally was to recognize that as her situation improved, and it did, how her preferred future became less restricted and more positive.

RECAP: CO-CREATING PREFERRED FUTURES

In this chapter we have looked at how we use the miracle question (whether qualified or unqualified) to establish a preferred future with the client, how we spend time eliciting the detail of what that preferred future looks like and the importance of recognizing that. Preferred futures are about moving towards something, not away from something. They are about life beyond and instead of the problem not life tied to a problem past.

PERSONAL REFLECTION

Thinking about your own preferred future, say 10 years from now, imagine you wake up and things are how you want them to be. You open your eyes. Where are you? Who is there on that day? What is your job? Who are your friends? What are your hobbies and interests? What are you looking forward to?

TRY THIS

Ask the same questions as in the personal reflection section above to three colleagues or friends, announcing to them that this is an experiment to help you feel more comfortable about certain therapeutic questions. Get them to visualize this day for no less than 10 minutes. If you get stuck, simply ask 'What else?' or 'And what else would you notice?'

KEY TERMS USED IN THIS CHAPTER

Miracle question, wonderful question, qualified, preferred future, visualization.

SUGGESTED FURTHER READING

de Shazer, S., Dolan, Y., with Korman, H., Trepper, T., McCollum, E., & Berg, I. K. (2007). *More than miracles: the state of the art of solution-focused brief therapy*. London: The Haworth Press.

Chapters 3 and 4 of this book are of special note. I particularly like the way the authors illustrate different possible answers to the miracle question and the therapist response. I could not hope to better their description in this book, so I merely point you in the direction of these chapters. Chapter 4 is concerned with the 'Miracle Scale' and is worth reading to understand in more depth the thinking – dare I say, the theory – behind the scaling questions and the relation to the miracle question.

7

END OF SESSIONS, TASKS AND FEEDBACK

LEARNING OUTCOMES

By the end of this chapter the reader will:

- Be clear about the origins, purpose and applications of:

  - The break (if used) in SFBT
  - The use of therapist feedback/message to the client and the invitation for the client to feed back to the therapist

- Know how to end an SF session, including the setting of tasks
- Appreciate how task-setting differs from behavioural models of therapy while also recognizing the commonalities
- Recognize the different types of task and purpose

ENDINGS OF SESSIONS/MEETINGS

Therapists traditionally use a therapy hour or 50 minutes. I do not know why – tradition and established practice seem to dominate and stalk the therapy world. This tradition, as with many other areas utilized in therapy, is not necessarily adhered to in SFBT. In fact, if a convenient point in the meeting is reached, such as a point of realization or resolution, the meeting may well end there. 'It can be beneficial to end on a strong, positive note' (O'Connell, 1998: 27). Indeed, to ensure that someone spends the full 50 minutes or hour in the therapy room when it is not needed seems to be very therapist-led and opposed to SFBT principles and beliefs. Someone once said to me that keeping a client beyond the helpful time is 'false imprisonment'.

I have worked a lot with young people, especially teenagers, in my practice, and a full hour in a therapy room is certainly not the norm. It is desirable, in my opinion, to state from the outset to a client what time is available, and clarify that this is a maximum time and that should they feel they want to end the session earlier, then that is OK.

What is important is that the end of the session is determined by an agreed outcome either at the start of the session or during the session.

THE BREAK AND FEEDBACK IN SFBT

Throughout the session there have been hundreds or thousands of words spoken, scales noted, exceptions discovered, and so on. One of the purposes of the break is to give yourself and the client a short period of reflection. Another reason is that it indicates the closing segment of the meeting to the client. The other main reason is to prepare to give the feedback. While it may not be appropriate or practical to physically leave the room for the break, it is possible to take a 'pause in proceedings' in the room.

There are definitely the roots of systemic family therapy in this pause in proceedings, where often a team observing from behind a mirror would be consulted at the end of a therapy session and an agreed message would be fed back to the client(s) by that team. The Milwaukee team certainly did this, and many SF teams still do.

I am going to differ slightly from many SF brief therapists by stating that I do not like to leave a room for two reasons. First, it seems a little rude to me. I have been left in a room while professionals attend to others or go and get something and it does not always sit right with clients, although certainly most therapists who do this do check in with the client(s) first. Secondly, the idea of going off and consulting with others, before 'delivering' a message, seems to me to be a little at odds with the non-expert position of SFBT.

I do, however, like the idea of a small pause in proceedings, and I think it can be beneficial to do this in the room with the client so they can see you referring back to notes, so they can have a chance to reflect too, and so they do not feel 'abandoned'.

During this pause for reflection the therapist should be referring to their notes to look for relevant points to feedback to the client (Duncan, Ghul & Mousley, 2007). The notes, once reflected upon, give the therapist a clear framework for a short, structured period of feedback to the client. This feedback should not be a long, observational lecture – in fact, I would recommend no more than two or three minutes – and the feedback should do several things.

Feedback should emphasize the positives

Do not be so positive as to be patronizing (this is a skill in itself), but do look at what has been said by the client that is positive, and do relate back any positive movements, situations or ideas highlighted by the client and by you, the therapist. Above all, reflect back the fact that the client is coming to the meeting and is working hard, that this is positive in itself and is a good starting point. One can also be clear at this stage that the bulk of the work will be done outside the therapy room. In this respect, we might also reflect on any positives that have happened prior to our meeting with the client, as this strengthens the message that work continues outside the therapy room.

Feedback should emphasize the exceptions

If exceptions are discovered (and they should be), highlight them, emphasize them and amplify them. Clients may have taken little notice of them when they happened and may not even realize they are making them. Leaving it until the end of the session to discuss them can be extremely powerful. This can also lead to the client trying to turn random exceptions into deliberate ones and/or recognizing that they have intentionally made exceptions happen before and can do this again.

Feedback should not be false

While this should not need explaining to most therapists, I have often heard those new to solution talk relating, in the end-of-session feedback, positives and exceptions that were simply not there. Making false positives and statements of hope is detrimental to the client. This must not happen. People must not live in a therapeutic bubble of hope, only to feel deflated when they leave a session.

Feedback should reflect the session, including ways forward

It is important to summarize the meeting, highlighting the key points so that the client can recognize the story as their own. It is equally important to reflect on any agreed ways forward, especially outside the meeting, so that the client understands that they are not tied to the therapy room for the solutions. It is useful, where appropriate, to highlight any scale points and any future scale points. It is extremely important, in my opinion, to not talk in jargon at this point. We should reflect back the client's own words where we can and reflect back what we have heard and learnt from them.

Feedback should be encouraging and give praise where appropriate

Compliments, of course, are not just given in the end-of-session feedback, although they should be included in this feedback if appropriate. It is good for people to hear that they have done well despite difficult situations, it is generally good for people to hear that they have worked hard, and it is good for people to hear that they can be in control of elements of their future. Not everyone is happy with praise and compliments straight away and sometimes clients have to 'learn' how to accept them. So do not shower people with praise where it is inappropriate or you sense that clients are not receptive.

Below are two examples of client feedback, including Sally's first session.

CASE EXAMPLE: GIVING FEEDBACK

Therapist: Well Joe, I'd like to say that I was impressed that you managed to get here at all as it is your third day of withdrawal. It is obvious to me that you are really serious about stopping. Well done. I was also really pleased to hear your descriptions of how things have improved between you and your partner, and was quite touched to hear how much you realize you both mean to each other. I think you have made an excellent start in what seem to be very difficult circumstances. You mentioned that in order to move one point up the scale you needed to tell your parents what has been happening, because you didn't want to lie. I recognize that's going to be difficult and that you need to think about the right time, and I admire your self-awareness in that area.

SALLY

Therapist: I have made some notes Sally, as I said I would, and I would like to tell you what I think happened today, though of course I may have got some, or all, of it wrong. I would welcome you telling me about that in a minute. Is that OK? [*she nods*]. You have clearly been going through a really hard time of it, and still are. You have had a life-changing thing happen and it has meant you can no longer do many of the things you used to. You somehow manage to get through each day, you try to put on a brave face for Mick, and you have also put the welfare of your dog above your own by letting your sister take care of him for now. You clearly think about others, even your doctor, who you do not want to let down. So you carry on, even though you are not convinced things can get better. And yet, I was really interested to hear that sometimes, such as when Mick is at home, you don't feel quite as bad as he sometimes manages to cheer you up a little bit, and it was nice to hear about your seaside trip. You have made the decision to stay alive, although you have considered not staying alive, and you have made the effort to come today and allowed me to work with you. I thank you for that and hope I can be helpful.

I would always then ask if a client had any comments to feed back to me and whether they wanted to see me again. I would then discuss a between-session task. Although some practitioners do the task-setting before end-of-session feedback, personally I do not think there is any right or wrong way to do this.

BETWEEN-SESSION TASKS (BST)

With any therapy we (client and therapist) would hope to see some improvement or at least some movement in a client's situation. These next small steps can be asked in terms of scaling or in terms of thoughts and feelings or, in some cases, in concrete and practical terms by negotiating a task between client/therapist meetings.

Not all SF practitioners still employ between-session tasks; I do. The client's life outside the sessions is their real life, and is therefore most important – more so than the time spent in the counselling room. We see someone for 50–60 minutes per week, but they have another 23 hours of that day to fill and another six days when we are not there. We should, in my opinion, therefore encourage people to do things that will benefit them between sessions.

I agree with Lipchik (2002) that a task should be seen as more of a 'suggestion' offered by therapist, a suggestion that a client has complete freedom to accept or reject. They may well suggest something else in its place. There is a skill to encouraging between-session tasks with a client and it comes down to being humble and, in some ways, tentative. A suggestion from the therapist should relate to something the client has mentioned, even in passing, and generally it should come only when a client has little or no idea of a task themselves, or is unable to articulate one. For example:

Therapist:	So, you have mentioned that you would see moving up one point on your scale would be you noticing that you had a bit more of an interest outside your home. Do you have any ideas of what you might do that could help towards this one point up on your scale?
Client:	Erm, no, not really, er, I can't think of anything. [*pause*] No.
T:	Some people have found it helpful to actually go out more. You mentioned that you used to play pool in a pub and a pool club. Could you maybe try that again, would that be helpful?
C:	No, not the pub, too many people, too noisy, but I suppose I could go to the pool club with my mate. It's quite dark and not very busy in the mornings.

From this particular point I gauged with the client, using scales, how likely he was to go and play pool, highlighted and praised his thinking about going when it was less busy and got him to 'work through' each step of the event, visualizing it. He reported back at our next meeting that it was successful.

SALLY

Discussing a task with Sally proved difficult at the first session as she was clearly exhausted at the end and could not think of anything she could do that would help. We therefore agreed a simple task of her noticing any time over the next two weeks (her timeframe for our next session) that she noticed, even for a minute, that she was higher on her scale than 0 out of 10, and what was happening at that point.

If we look a little further into between-session tasks, referred to in notes as BST, they should always be:

Negotiated: They should never be 'given' or handed down (in a hierarchical sense) by the therapist, for if you set a task and someone does not achieve it, who has failed? I am not opposed to 'suggesting' something, based on what we have learnt in the session at that point, as mentioned previously, however, you need to make it clear that it is entirely up to the client, and if they have a better idea, we should go with that. For example:

T: You mentioned earlier that you would like to see the exhibition at the local gallery. As a suggestion, and feel free to say if it is too much, why not give it a go?

C: I don't know, it might be busy, it might be a bit too scary at the moment, though I did notice that they are open from 10am. There might not be many people in then. No, I don't think I could.

T: OK, no one is making you. I just suggested it because you were not able to think of something you could do to get out, and you did say that you wanted to see this exhibition because of the mining history and that.

C: I'd probably be OK to look at the window display as it is all along the front. Then, if I was OK, I could go in. What do you think?

T: I think that sounds like a good idea. You would be getting out of the house, you would be seeing some of the exhibition, and if you felt up to it, you could always take that next step. Yeah, it sounds good to me, wish I'd have thought of it.

While this client did not feel able to complete a suggested task, they clearly wanted to do 'something' and it was important to them that I acknowledged their idea. It is also important that as the therapist I was able to take a step back from my 'suggestion'. Had they attempted and failed, it would after all have been partially my failure for suggesting too big a task. Incidentally, this client did go into the gallery, which they excitedly told me about on their next visit.

Realistic and achievable: There is absolutely no point in setting someone up to fail. If a client is using 10 bags of heroin daily and they suggest that they are going to stop, just like that, after seeing you, it is your job not to dismiss this as an idea, but to explore the reality of achieving that, and relate it back to their 'scale'. Maybe cutting down by one bag per day this week is more achievable.

I once saw a client who, since the death of his wife, had not been to a social event for over a decade. He was terrified by the prospect of even talking to a neighbour. At the end of his first session he was so enthused that he told me he was going to go to a dating dance in a big local city. I gently asked him if he succeeded in doing this where would it put him on his scale of being 'outgoing and confident'. He replied 8 out of 10, yet he was currently at 1 out of 10. Rather than dismiss his idea out of hand I gently enquired what 2 out of 10 looked like. He responded that maybe he should at least say hello to his neighbour before heading off on further adventures. I agreed with him of course and complimented him on his insight.

Measurable: The task should always relate to the scale: 'So if you managed to go until evening without a drink, that would put you at a 2 on the scale? OK, is there anything that you could do that might help this to happen?'

We need to recognize here that a between-session task is often related to behavioural change, or at the very least a new behaviour happening. This is perhaps why some SFBT practitioners do not like a BST – it is too close to other behaviouralist therapies, such as CBT. However, if someone is coming to see the therapist with change in mind, surely that change has to start somewhere? In addition, if you, as a therapist, feel uncomfortable with behavioural task-setting, there is always the option of simply getting clients to 'notice' or observe times when things are getting better and notice what is helping (see 'viewing' below).

Related to the therapeutic input: If the between-session task is related to what you have both been talking about, it becomes more 'real', it is more 'shared', in understanding at least, and can be 'visited', if appropriate, at the next session, should there be one.

MORE ON TASKS

Tasks can be broadly split into 'viewing' tasks and 'doing' tasks or, as de Shazer (1985) and De Jong and Berg (2002) describe them, observational tasks and behavioural tasks.

Personally, I tend to suggest or negotiate 'viewing' tasks in first meetings – not always, but often. The act of viewing or noticing is often less onerous than someone having to 'do' something, so, in my opinion, is more likely to be successful. If, however, when asked, a client responds in a behavioural way – 'I would have to do XXX' – knowing that we are working to the client's agenda, I would encourage this.

If a client is talking about being depressed and bored yet they have mentioned that they have friends who have offered to pop round, why not suggest they try seeing those friends, especially if they have commented that this has been useful in the past? Or, as a viewing task, why not ask them what the first sign of being less depressed or a bit happier might be? What would they notice? What would others notice?

When the client says they feel good now that they are not drinking, why not get them to think about noticing all the smells, sounds and tastes that are different now. Again, I will emphasize here that clients should ideally set their own tasks. We should make suggestions only where they cannot, and certainly not at every session – we should be encouraging that autonomy.

If small, achievable tasks are set, the client is more likely to achieve them. If a client does not achieve a small task, it is less damaging than if it were a major life task. Tasks can be:

Noticing things

You can use the following interventions or similar. For example:

'I wonder what you will notice between now and next week that tells you that you have moved slightly up that scale?'

'So, between now and the next time we meet, it might be useful for you to notice all the times, no matter how brief, that you feel a little better than 2 out of 10, and what was happening at that time that helped. Was it a certain song on the radio, a sunny day, a friend telephoning? Do you think you could do that?'

'As you have told me that you are going to try and see the positive side to things in your team, I have an idea. Play the detective and see what positive things you can notice, at least one per team member. I'd be interested to see if that is in any way helpful.'

'It would be great if you did notice any time at work when people tell you that you have done something well, like last week, when you told me that your colleague commented on how helpful you had been with her computer issue.'

Writing things down

Often people are asked in therapy to write down problems, triggers and ways of overcoming them in diaries. A drink diary is a good example. I might ask clients if they could write down positive things that have happened, or a positive thought diary even. This is something that has been very successful in working with clients who present with depression and/or anxiety. Often clients will come back with many positive thoughts that they have had, or positive moments they have noticed. Dolan's letter from the future (Dolan, 2000) is a great example of a solution focused positive writing task.

Going somewhere

Somebody might benefit from a between-session task of visiting someone, getting out for a day, going shopping, visiting a park. This can be related particularly well to a 'mood scale'. You can ask people where they place themselves on a scale of 0–10 in mood (where 10 is the best) on a day when they do not get out, and on the same scale when they have managed to get out and/or do something.

Talking

Numerous times I have had people relate to me how a significant other 'does not know how I feel', only to be told that they had not discussed those feelings. The therapeutic process sometimes helps people to be able to have these conversations outside the therapy room and this should be encouraged where appropriate.

One client once told me that he was extremely isolated and talked to no one. On further exploration, of course, he talked to some people although those conversations were purely functional. He and I negotiated a between-session task of him going into a local community centre and simply asking for a leaflet on evening activities. Not only did he do this, but he also spoke at length to a worker in the centre and that very week went to a book group. His particular scale point moved from 0 to 5 in one week.

Having fun

While initially this may sound a frivolous task it is surprising how many people in the therapy room have forgotten how to have fun. One man I worked with was complaining that he and his wife could never agree on an activity so ended up doing nothing but staying in. I suggested that he and his partner wrote down three activities on three pieces of paper that they wanted to do. Each partner had to include an activity that neither had suggested before. The pieces of paper were to be folded and put in a container or hat. Each partner would take out one in turn and they would try each activity over the coming weeks in the order in which they were selected.

This client told me at our next meeting that they had indeed done this task and had both been in hysterics at the 'unknown' tasks. He had suggested a tank-driving day and she had suggested going to a naturist beach. I should add that over time they completed these as well as their other, less unpredictable tasks, such as a cinema visit and a walk in a park. I bumped into the client some years later in town and he told me that not only were he and his partner still putting ideas in a hat, but that they had suggested this to some friends who were having marital problems.

Work-related tasks

One of my clients related to me that all the people in his place of employment were cold towards him, that they did not like him. He proceeded to give me lots of examples to illustrate this. We agreed an 'experiment' to 'prove' this once and for all. He was to say 'good morning' or hello to every person in his workplace, for a week and gauge their reaction to him. He came the next week telling me how everyone had changed towards him and were much friendlier. He also stated that he could not work out why until he had the lightbulb moment of realizing that he could change things.

Relationship-related tasks

A client told me when we were talking about how she would notice that things were improving 'If me and my husband talked about my depression, but he doesn't dare because he doesn't want to upset me. I suppose I could let him know that I am OK to talk about it, that might help. What do you think?' I replied that I thought it was a good idea if she thought that. She announced one evening over dinner 'It is OK to talk about my depression you know, it's not like you are going to make it any worse'.

FINDING OUT ABOUT TASK COMPLETION

I very, very rarely ask about task completion in follow-up sessions for a very simple reason. If we do, then we risk making the session hierarchical and focused on the task completion. Where therapists have asked about task completion in the past, it has had negative outcomes. There have been occasions where clients have stopped coming because they do not want to 'let the therapist down'. There have also been occasions where clients have lied about task completion as they do not want to be seen as failing. There is a balance here because if one does not ask about task completion we can risk appearing to be disinterested in our client's progress. So there are ways of approaching this, including the following:

- Let the client know that you will not normally ask about task completion but invite them to mention it if they want to when they come next time, thereby preparing them for the question.
- Say nothing and wait to see if the client mentions the task.
- Ask the client at the end of subsequent sessions, when you would normally agree a between-session task, if setting a task previously was useful.

SALLY

Sally mentioned in her second or third session that her husband had paid for a spa treatment for her and that some classical music had been playing and that she felt for a moment at 5 out of 10 on her scale. On the surface, that was a great observation and enthused me as a therapist. However, this would be a good point to illustrate the SF position of not being the expert on the client. When I expressed my enthusiasm to Sally, she told me that she felt even worse after the spa treatment as she had 'realized' that her life would only have fleeting moments of 'being all right' but never lasting joy. Undaunted, I did revisit this fleeting moment several times in that and subsequent sessions, and this proved fruitful later on.

ENDING THE SESSION

We always ask if a client wants to come again in SFBT. This will be explored further in the next chapter. Whether they do or don't, we have rounded off that session's work with feedback and task-setting. At that point, we have completed our work.

RECAP: END OF SESSIONS, TASKS AND FEEDBACK

This chapter recognizes that, like any therapeutic meeting, the solution focused session must come to an end. We ensure that we have listened carefully and established a preferred future by feeding back what we have heard to the client. We check with the client, by asking them, if that feedback accurately reflected the session. We also negotiate a task outside therapy that will help the client move towards their preferred future, by moving up their scale(s). We have recognized that not all SF brief therapists employ between-session tasks.

PERSONAL REFLECTION

Think about the progression of your career or an interest or hobby. Think about where you are now (scale point) and where you would like to be (scale point). Think about how you will notice that you have moved slightly towards that end scale point and if there is anything you could do or notice that would help in that progression. Set yourself a task related to that scale point. Check in with yourself later to see if it worked. Have you moved up the scale?

TRY THIS

With the next client you see, make some notes of key points throughout your meeting, and when you have about 10 minutes to go until the end of the session, or if there is an appropriate pause in your conversation, suggest something like this to your client:

> Is it OK with you if I just take a moment to reflect on what we have both said, and then tell you what I think has happened today. I need to be sure that I am on the right track, so I would appreciate you letting me know that.

Then do just that. After the session think to yourself how that felt for you and the client. Did it feel like a good closure to the session?

> ## KEY TERMS USED IN THIS CHAPTER
>
> End of session, feedback, message, task, between-session tasks, completion, viewing, doing, noticing.

> ## SUGGESTED FURTHER READING
>
> Dolan, Y. (2000). *Beyond survival: living well is the best revenge*. London: BT Press.
> Tasks and exercises form a large part of this book and while the primary focus is on recovering from sexual abuse, many of the tasks are adaptable to SFBT as between-session tasks.

8

SUBSEQUENT SESSIONS AND CLOSURES IN SFBT

LEARNING OUTCOMES

By the end of this chapter the reader will:

- Appreciate that each session in SFBT is different and not fully formulated until the client arrives and clarifies their agenda
- Understand that each session keeps with the client-led focus and original goals
- Be able to stay 'on track' in subsequent client meetings (i.e. after the first)
- Appreciate how subsequent sessions illustrate and measure client progress
- Understand the concept of 'closure' in SFBT

SECOND AND SUBSEQUENT SESSIONS IN SFBT

The EBTA protocol and many proponents of SFBT would start a second and subsequent sessions of SFBT with 'What's got better since we last met?' or a variation of a question like that. The purpose of this line of questioning is to establish from the outset a framework of looking for the parts of the solution(s) that have happened already since the last session. This builds on a foundation for recognizing what is working, amplifying it and exploring it further.

If a client answers with 'nothing', it is worth waiting a second or two to see if they self-challenge, expand or clarify. One might then ask how they have coped or managed with nothing getting better, or even ask if that means nothing has worsened. Remember, no change is always better than things getting worse. If a client answers that things have indeed got worse, it is useful, again, to look at how they have coped with this.

On a personal level, I like to 'soften' this opening with something like:

'It has been some time since we last met and some things would have got better, some would have stayed about the same and some things might have got worse. Would you mind if we started by you telling me what you have noticed that has been better?'

Once the opening question has been asked, the format for the meeting will depend on the answer. Clearly, however, the meeting should also address the preferred future best hopes, and the goals agreed at the first meeting. The therapist should then check where the client is on their scale and explore any changes between their current scale point and the previous one. In earlier chapters I have discussed the importance of exploring and discussing pre-session change. The idea of asking about what has got better is very much, in my opinion, a follow-on from this concept and an exploration of what I will call 'between-session change'. The assumption, however, is that some things will have improved, so it is not simply an exploration but is rather more defined than that.

This initial exploration of any changes since the last meeting can seem, for both therapist and client, a little daunting at first. However, it is worth persevering with as it helps both client and therapist focus on and home in on the little changes that are happening. As with all therapeutic interventions, there is a caveat here. If the client finds a line of questioning uncomfortable, we should back off. I would then ask something like: 'So, since I last saw you, has anything changed at all that you think it would be useful for us to discuss here today.' Whatever they then say we need to determine how discussing that would be useful.

The important point to note here is that, unlike most other therapies, we will not have already formulated a set of responses, a progression from the last intervention. After the initial question 'What's got better?' and a checking-in of where people are, the remainder of the session very much depends on the client's lead. Some SF brief therapists call this 'leading from behind'.

ASKING ABOUT TASK COMPLETION

This was discussed initially in the previous chapter. I would never start a session by asking about task completion, unless of course the client had previously directed me to. Doing so would be a behavioural approach and could lead to the client being defensive and 'guilty' about non-completion. This does not sit well with the SF principle of client-directed therapy and a collaborative approach. Further, it risks alienating the client to the extent that they do not attend further sessions for fear of being 'told off' (literally or internally) for task failure. There is here, as with all therapeutic interventions, a balance to be had. If we do not ask about task completion, it is possible (though I have only rarely experienced this) that a client feels we are not paying due attention to task completion.

However, the line of questioning around 'What's got better?' often invites the client to report back on their task. If a client reports back on the task of their own accord, then by all means work with that. In my experience, clients do often volunteer this information. There are three possible client responses concerning task completions:

1   They did not attempt the task.
2   They attempted the task and it was partially successful.
3   They attempted the task and it was wholly successful.

They did not attempt the task

If the client relates that they did not attempt the task, they will have a good reason for this. They may have been scared, they may not have had an opportunity to attempt the task, external events may have prevented the task attempt. They may even have simply forgotten to try the task. The SFBT response here should be, first, to establish if the task is (in the client's view) able to be attempted again, and if that is indeed desirable. There should be an acknowledgement that the task was properly thought through. Maybe the task was too big? If this was the case, we should acknowledge our part in that and try to negotiate a smaller, more manageable task. We should also point out that not everyone completes tasks at their first attempt, or even at the second attempt. We should praise the client for their honesty. We might also ask the client if task-setting is something they wish to continue with. If it is not, then we might ask at this and subsequent sessions if they have noticed or done anything that was helpful between sessions – this is a kind of retrospective task acknowledgement. It may also be helpful at this point to explore any exceptions or improvements 'despite' not completing the task. I have done this and commented to clients 'Oh, so you did not need that task after all'.

They attempted the task and it was partially successful

There are NO failures. Let me give you an example. Pete, who had a phobia about eating in front of people, set himself a task of eating a small cake in a café with his girlfriend present. He had never done this before. On his return meeting he reported to me that he was 'gutted' that he had failed. He in fact reported that he was at a lower place on his scale as a result of this 'perceived' failure. Initially, it was tempting to be empathic and validate his feelings of failure, comfort him and not focus on the failed task. However, SF brief therapists do not do this. Yes, we validate feelings, and then we explore further to look for what did work, but we do not focus on what didn't work.

   On further exploration, I found out that Pete had managed to go into a café and *did* drink a coffee. He ordered a cake but could not eat it, so his girlfriend did. My response to him was as follows:

'So Pete, you went to a café, even though you were scared. You opened the door and you found a seat, you sat down – all of these things were new to you. You then ordered a coffee and a cake, you drank the coffee and your girlfriend got the gift of a cake. Well done you.'

He responded by saying that he had not looked at it like that and was quite pleased that he had managed to get into a café at all. No failures then!

Joanne set herself a task of not eating chocolate for a whole week and managed three days. When we next met, rather than allow her to self-berate about the four days when she had 'given in', we concentrated on what she had done that was helpful in the three days that she had managed to resist chocolate. She was genuinely surprised at this line of questioning and after much discussion she realized that going a week without chocolate was not something she actually wanted. Once she had given in, she felt there was little point in continuing to try as she had failed. With her new found realization she set herself a task of going three days without chocolate the following week, eating chocolate for one day, and resisting a further three. She succeeded in this – after all, she was only repeating a previous success.

So the therapist's response here is to be gentle, to explore further and to find out what, if anything, did work and how that might be repeated. Above all, the focus should be on the partially successful part of the task completion, not on any parts that were not successful.

However, there is one instance where we might focus on the bits that were unsuccessful, and that is to highlight to the client, and acknowledge in the therapy room, that they have indeed tried. The 'attempting' of some tasks for some people can be a massive achievement in itself. We should never forget this.

They attempted the task and it was wholly successful

A client decided that they were going to make themselves wait 10 minutes before 'giving in' to each marijuana cigarette because their goal was to have more willpower (not just in this area). Not only did they do this, they succeeded in the time between therapy sessions in managing up to an hour before giving in to each joint, thus reducing their intake substantially.

Another client with a lift phobia set themselves a between-session task of going in a lift for one floor down with a friend. They reported back that not only had they done this, but they had made their friend travel up and down with them in the lift several times, and then they had done it alone.

One client who managed to travel for one stop on a bus between their first and second therapy session managed to take a whole bus journey – 'between 15 and 20 stops, I lost count' – between their second and third session.

There are many, many more examples of successful task completion, of going beyond the original task, and of self-setting new tasks. Our response as solution focused brief therapists should be to:

- Praise the client for their successes, exploring how they managed the task, what helped, and what they noticed and learned about themselves.
- Find out from them if further task-setting is useful and, if so, ensure that they take an increasing lead in task-setting as we step back.
- Find out what they and others have noticed as a result of successful task completion, not just about the task, but if other things have improved too.
- Acknowledge that not every task will be 100% successful, and that they have achieved the current/past tasks and any future events cannot take away from that.

All of these things could, and in my opinion should, be approached in a 'light' way, using humour where applicable, but not so lightly as to take anything away from the successes.

MORE ABOUT THE SECOND AND SUBSEQUENT SESSIONS

In the first meeting the therapist and client have established a focus for their work – their 'best hopes'. Hopefully they will have established a point on the scale where the client has been in relation to where they want to be, and what the preferred future, once arrived at, will look like, including where on the same scale they would be.

After the initial opening (of the second and subsequent sessions), it can be useful to check in with the client that the focus remains the same and where they currently are on any previously discussed scales. At this point it is essential to examine what has happened that tells the client they are at a different point on the scale (if they are). For example:

Therapist: Lisa, when we saw each other last week you mentioned that you were at a 4 out of 10 on your scale related to how you were coping with the situation at work. Where are you today on that same scale?

Client: Maybe four and a half, or five? I dunno, I seem to have things in a bit more perspective, I think.

T: Really, now that interests me, what's different?

C: Well, it's like, I only work three days, so really I spend more time out of work, so I should enjoy that more, not worry so much about what happens when I'm there, it's only a job after all. I want things to be different there, but if I can't make that happen, it shouldn't creep into my home life like it has been doing, should it?

T: Gosh, sounds like you have been doing a lot of thinking and that has been helping you. I'm glad to hear that. What would be a useful use of your time here today? What should we talk about?

Asking the question 'What is different?' or 'What difference has that made?' or variations of this, is an extremely useful SF intervention. It is a real skill to remember to use it and hone it. Likewise, asking 'What else?' when a client starts to recount things either in responding to the miracle question, when noticing differences, or in any other client-led conversation is also a real skill. Asking 'What else?' invites the client to keep noticing and keep talking:

T: And after you got home, you noticed that you felt calmer. Good. What else?
C: I was pleased, really pleased that I done it. I said I would and I did.
T: So, you were calmer, and pleased, and so you should be, and what else?
C: Well, I wanted to tell people. I phoned my mum, told her I'd been to town. She was dead chuffed [really happy], didn't believe it at first, then that made me feel even happier.

Note that all I did was to repeat the client's own words and add 'and what else?' There was no interpretation, formulation or analysis; simply the client's own words.

SALLY

After about nine or ten meetings with Sally, of me establishing how she was managing and/or coping, and several supervision sessions, where I expressed my frustration about 'not getting anywhere', my supervisor asked me what I thought Sally was getting out of coming to see me. On reflection, my response was that I was not sure. Maybe that Sally was happy to just be heard. My supervisor asked me how, in an SF way, I could move this on. The truth is I did not know, so I decided to trust in the model and just keep on for a while, though I realized that I had not asked Sally at the last meeting, that week, if that meeting was useful to her. I decided to start with that at the next meeting. So after asking Sally if anything had improved for her, to which she replied no, I asked her:

T: I'm really sorry Sally, I forgot to ask you at the end of the last session if that meeting was useful or not, and I guess what I am also asking you is how you will know that these meetings are being of use to you? You keep coming back.
S: Oh they are useful. It gives me a chance to talk to someone without risking them being upset, like Mick would be. No offence but it doesn't matter if I moan on to you.
T: No offence taken, Sally, I can assure you. [At this point Sally smiled.] So supposing these sessions were to be even more helpful than you just talking to someone without upsetting them, supposing they actually moved you up that feelings' scale we talked about, what do you think we could talk about here that might help in that?
S: You know, it's interesting, because I actually look forward to coming here. It gets me out of the house and gives me something to think about when I get home, so I suppose it is helping [she stops and looks puzzled]. I have just realized, I said I look forward to something. How sad is that? I look forward

> to seeing my therapist. Oh god, I have become a therapy junkie. [*Then she laughed properly, the first time I had seen this.*] Who would have thought it?
>
> T: I'm not sure you're a therapy junkie, no more than I am, I guess [*we both laughed*]. Apart from this, then, have you noticed yourself, by accident, looking forward to anything else?
>
> S: Not really, but I forgot to tell you. I put some music on the other day, some Irish music while I was cleaning up, doing the washing up. My good foot started tapping.
>
> T: Now that sounds like a pretty significant thing, would you agree?
>
> S: Are you going to ask me about the scale now [*she smiled*]?
>
> T: Should I?
>
> S: Well, thinking about it now, it was a bit brighter, listening to some music, and I did not feel as sad about not being able to play the fiddle either – just realized that too. Isn't that interesting?
>
> T: Very. OK then, where on the scale were you when washing up and listening to Irish music?
>
> S: You're not going to believe this – probably about 7, for a good 20 minutes I reckon.
>
> T: Wow, that is something.

For Sally, and indeed myself, this was a breakthrough point. I carried on seeing Sally for a long time and there were ups and downs. She eventually started to learn to play the piano, after discovering that while her crooked finger and hand would not allow her to play the fiddle any more, she could manage the piano. This proved to be the turning point for her as she started going to piano lessons, started to enjoy herself more and to get out more. In fact, Sally told me that she had always wanted to learn to play the piano as a child and had never had time to do so.

I stopped seeing Sally when she decided that coming to therapy reminded her that she had had a problem. She no longer wanted to associate her life with that problem. We had a very emotional last meeting where she thanked me for giving her her life back. I told her she had grabbed it back herself and I thanked her for persevering with me, and told her that I had learnt an awful lot from her. I learnt that I had to stay with the client and keep to their pace. Of course I already knew this, but Sally had a very different pace from many of the clients I had been working with. I learnt that SFBT can be used in more than just a few sessions and that it is important to trust the model and use the SF skills over and over. Don't give up. I learnt, or relearnt, that the client has the answers. We have to be skilful in asking the right questions and humble enough to accept when we get it wrong and try a different question. I also learnt, from a personal perspective, that using SFBT in instances that were/are described as 'hopeless' or not 'appropriate' (as one colleague described SFBT with Sally) is possible. Sally gave me great confidence in my therapy journey and gave me great hope in the powers of human adaptability and recovery.

So, it is important to keep focused in the second and subsequent meetings with clients, be they two meetings or twenty. It is important to revisit any scales, and it is important to constantly 'check in' that you are on the right track with the work. It is also important, no matter how many meetings you have, to constantly revisit the client's initial best hopes and goals in coming to see you, to gently persevere with lines of questioning that are helpful, to listen for, and highlight, any exceptions and differences, and to establish and check in constantly what it is that is helpful about coming to see you and how that relates to their life outside the therapy room. Most of all, it is vital that you recognize that any session could be the last. Do not leave things 'hanging'. Complete each meeting with a closure session whether it is feedback, a negotiated task or simply a summary of that meeting's work/discussion.

There are, of course, differences between closing an individual session in SFBT and therapy 'closures' when you finish your work with a client.

INDIVIDUAL SESSION CLOSURES

Each session, then, has an end and we need to establish whether people want and/or need to return. We do not assume that they do. We might also ask at the end of each session:

- 'Would it be useful for you to come again?'
- 'Do you feel you need to see me again?'

We should not assume that the client needs or even wants to see us again. They may have got all they needed from that one session, or we may have been of no use at all. We won't know unless we 'check in':

- 'Did you find this session useful? If so, how?'
- 'What do you feel you have got from this session?'
- 'Was this session what you expected? Could it have gone differently? If so, how?'

I generally ask a client to 'score' the usefulness of the session on a scale from 0 (no use at all) to 10 (extremely useful). I ask them what they think was useful and not so useful, and ask them how they would know if the next session (presuming we have one) was even more useful.

ESTABLISHING A CLIENT–LED CLOSURE IN SFBT

In solution focused working we start thinking about endings from early on in the relationship. It is not our role to keep clients coming back, depending on us for their solutions. Quite the opposite, in fact. The less I am needed as an SF practitioner, the more the client is doing for themselves. This means that the client gets the sessions they need, and no more. This is something that all SF brief therapists hold dear: the less we do, and the quicker we do it, the more the client does.

This may seem quite challenging to those used to working in a problem focused model, where people may come to therapy for months, even years, in order to 'unravel' all the things that led to them having the problem in the first place. I have often heard other therapists say things like 'We are getting close to the root of the problem' or 'Until they face up to their past they will not be able to move on'. Solution focused brief therapists do not see much point in this. Surely, people come to us so that they can improve their lot, not rake over all the pain and turmoil in the therapy room. I am not saying that for some people this is not useful, it is just that in Solution Focused Brief Therapy, it's not what we do. What we look for are reasons for a closure, not a justification to keep a client coming.

We need to establish very early in the relationship what the client hopes to achieve from coming to see us, and how they will know when it is time to stop coming. To me, this is the very essence of 'being with' the client, not telling them what they have to do, when to come, when to stop coming. Self-determination and client-led therapy is the key here, and that cannot be achieved without some notion of what, when and how. We might ask:

'So tell me, how will you know when it's time to stop coming here?'

'What will be happening so that you don't need to come anymore?'

'So when you are drug-free for three months, is that when you know it will be OK to stop coming?'

'You mentioned that if you were able to sit down and discuss your issues with your wife you would not need to be seeing me. Can I check, then, if you do start sitting down and discussing things with your wife, you would think it is time to not come here anymore?'

It is essential at this point to establish a clear 'vision' for the ending for two reasons. First, so that we have a clear end in mind and as we approach that end the client is aware of it coming and that their goal and/or purpose for coming to see the therapist is coming to an end. Secondly, we want the client to be autonomous and independent as quickly as they can, and not 'needing' us. If we do not agree a closure point, then we run the risk of the client feeling abandoned and/or presenting other issues to work on as they feel only therapy can help.

We are used to getting what we need in other areas of our lives, so why should therapy be different? When we go to the bank to draw out some money, we get the money and leave. When we have a cold and take a linctus for a sore throat, we do not continue taking it when the throat is better. When our vehicle goes to the workshop to have an exhaust repaired, we do not leave it there, just in case something else goes wrong!

Establishing goals and times to stop coming can be extremely powerful for the client. I once saw a man who had been 'in therapy' since he was 12 (he was 34 years old when he came to see me). He had multiple personalities (over 20) which he used to deal with different situations: 'David' was good at his job, 'Pedro' was able to socialize in the pub. Each personality had different traits that helped my client cope in different situations. On asking what he hoped to achieve in therapy, he stated that he had seen dozens of therapists and that he could not get rid of the personalities. I asked him if that is what he wanted, to 'get rid' of the personalities. He responded that he thought it wasn't right to have all these personalities and asked me what I thought. My response was that I did not know. All I knew was that I wanted his time spent with me to be useful. He replied that therapy had never been useful up to that point.

> T: OK Stephen, is it all right if I call you Stephen? [*He nodded.*] Supposing I was to be the last therapist you saw, and somehow you got what you needed from coming here, and you made the decision that you no longer needed to come, have you thought about how you might know when it would be time to stop?
>
> C: Nope, no, not really. What do you mean? That the personalities went?
>
> T: I don't know, is that when you would not need to see a therapist, when the personalities went? What would be different then, if they did go?
>
> C: I don't know, really I don't. They have always been there. I might miss them [*laughs*].

In fact, we established together that having the personalities was not actually a problem for Stephen and he used them to cope with different situations. There were no malevolent personalities and they did not pose a danger to himself or others. What Stephen was in fact doing was 'naming' different ways that he coped with different situations. The main problem he had was constantly trying to rid himself of these personalities as everyone (professional and personal) seemed to tell him that this was what he needed to do.

He stopped coming to see me after five sessions. We had agreed that his time to stop coming would be when he decided for himself whether or not he wanted to be rid of the personalities. He realized that it was his decision alone. In fact, he decided that he did not want to get rid of his personalities as they served him well. He realized for the first time in his life that his personalities were a part of him and that the only 'problem' was that others saw it as a problem. He no longer did. As a postscript to this, someone in the psychology department made a statement that 'He'll be back'. I worked in the department for a further three years without seeing Stephen re-referred.

When I talk about endings in training sessions I am often asked how I will know when it is time for a client to stop coming. My answers are as follows.

It is time to stop coming if the client wants to stop coming

If someone does not want to come any more, for whatever reason, that is good enough. The one exception here is that of mandated clients. Some people 'have' to come whether they want to or not. Our task in these cases is to make the mandatory time spent with us as useful as it can be for the client, while acknowledging the mandatory nature of the meetings.

If a client wants to stop coming because you are not providing a good service, you will only know that if they tell you, and they may only tell you if you ask. Our initial response here should be to try to make the service we offer more useful and more client-focused. However, we need to accept that some clients will not want to see us, period.

A client may not want to come any more for a whole host of other reasons and all are valid and up to the client. They may have got enough for now, they may want to take time out to pause and reflect, they may have something better to do than come to see you.

I do not hold to the theory that people are 'not ready' for therapy. This seems somewhat patronizing. I prefer to think that if clients are not getting what they want from you at that point, or if they have got all they need, the decision as to whether to come or not rests with them. Again, we need constantly to check in with the client to see what is helpful and what is not.

It is time to stop coming when their needs are better met elsewhere

So if someone comes to you as an SF practitioner and tells you that their best hopes for coming to see you is that they spend two years going over their childhood with you, you are not the right person. However, do not simply dismiss the client. Find out what you 'might' be able to achieve with them before ensuring they are referred to a more appropriate service, if applicable. If what they need is practical housing help, you are not the right person. If they tell you that they really need medication, you are not the right person. There are many other reasons why you may not be the right person for someone to see. My response would be to help them recognize where they might get the appropriate help and, if possible, facilitate that.

There are many occasions, however, when people's initially stated 'best hopes' do not seem to be within the remit of the solution focused approach, and sometimes we have to explore this further:

T: So, tell me what you hope to achieve by coming here. How might I be useful?

C: I tried to kill myself six months ago and I keep going over and over it. I need to find out why I did it, so I don't do it again.

T: So you haven't worked it out in the last six months?

C: No, I just keep thinking why, why did I do that?

T: How might it help you to know why you did this, do you think?

C: Then I would not try it again. I mean, if I knew, then I could work it all out and I would not, you know, do this to myself again.

T: I'm intrigued. So even though you haven't come up with the answer, you haven't worked it all out, you haven't tried again, since that time?

C: No, but I need to know why. I need some answers.

T: I am wondering, even though you don't have the answers, what has kept you from trying to kill yourself in those six months since you tried?

C: [*Pauses*] Dunno, I suppose that I have realized that things aren't quite so bad.

From this beginning, I went on to find out what was working for the client, even though the stated initial goals were not the same. Indeed, he had not thought about the six months he had not tried to harm himself prior to coming to therapy as he was fixated on what he thought was the issue and was unable, initially, to look beyond this.

Similarly, I have often got a response from drug- and alcohol-using clients that their stated goals were to find out why they kept using, or why they started in the first place. The point I am making here is that although many people express initial hopes and goals that may not seem appropriate to the solution focused approach, it does not hurt to explore further. After all, they are there, so make use of that time, and if you cannot meet their needs, then neither you nor they have lost anything and you can still refer them on. This is extremely important. We should not assume, because clients do not 'fit' our assumptions of how we can be helpful, that we cannot indeed be helpful.

I have heard therapists from different approaches state things like 'He wasn't really right for XXX therapy' or 'She was resistant', and to be fair, if the training one has had means that clients and client issues are viewed in this way that is perfectly acceptable to those therapists. An SF brief therapist will not view things in the same way, however. They will try to 'fit' the therapy to the client, not the client to the therapy.

It is time to stop coming when goals have been achieved

As I have already intimated, it is less likely for a client to develop a dependency on the SFBT practitioner, especially when working with people who already have a dependency on alcohol or drugs or something else. We try to enable people to get on with their lives, to function without the need to keep coming back to see the therapist. Therefore, when someone has reached their goals, whether it be getting a job, going to college, or tidying up the garden, this is the time to reflect back to the client that they have reached their goals and it is time to end the therapy.

Probably the two hardest parts of going to see a therapist, or indeed anyone from a helping profession, are going in the first place, and then deciding it is OK to stop going. We need to respect both 'events', and make it clear from the beginning that when goals are reached it is time to stop coming. If people are (quite understandably) reticent about stopping coming, there are a number of things we can do to help.

I often spend some time reflecting with the client how well they have done, pointing out all the things they have achieved (without me) that have got them to where they are. I might ask them to scale their confidence on a scale of 0 to 10 of continuing as they are, or getting even better, taking care to ask 'how' they will continue and 'what' they will do to keep that confidence. Wherever the client places themselves on the confidence scale (apart from 10), I will ask how they will know when they are one point higher on the scale and maybe what needs to happen to get them there.

It is time to stop coming when the scale target has been reached

As above, if the point on the scale that they were aiming for after the wonderful question is reached, it is time to stop coming. What is important about this rationale for closure, and the previous one, is that we recognize that it is the client's goals and/or scale points that determine a closure, not because we think they are ready or not. I once heard a drugs worker state: 'I know she has said she has reached her goals, but I'm not so sure. So I have asked her to come back and see me again in a few weeks.' To me, this is not only not trusting a client, it is actually overriding a client's wishes. It is even, I might propose, an abuse.

If a client states that their goals or scale point have been reached and a closure happens, there is nothing to stop them referring themselves again, but to keep them on just because the therapist feels it is right, to me, seems inappropriate in most cases. Again, there are some exceptions, such as when working with someone who still presents (an assessed) risk to themselves or others.

It is time to stop coming when things are 'good enough'

The initial scale point after the wonderful question or the initial 'goals' may not get reached. This does not mean that we have to keep going until they are; they may never be reached. What if the wonderful day included winning the lottery? We all have dreams, aspirations and preferred futures. I wanted to be a black belt in Aikido. I got a blue belt and that was good enough. I want Tottenham Hotspur to win the premiership this year, but the top three is good enough (we were fourth last season).

Seriously, when someone gets some way along their journey to being better, achieving some of the things they set out to do, sometimes that is enough for now. It is our job as SF workers to encourage our clients to continue on this journey independently. Good enough is good enough.

T: I was really pleased to hear all the stuff you have been telling me about your confidence coming back and that you are a lot less anxious most of the time. You told me some time ago that you wanted to go to Meadowhall [the big shopping mall], that then you would know you are better. How close on a scale of 0 to 10, with 10 being you can definitely do it, are you now?

C: Probably about 5, but it doesn't matter because I can go into town and get most things I need now. I don't really 'need' to go to Meadowhall. I might do one day, but even if I don't, I can still do loads of things now.

T: That you can, so, do you mind if we spend a little time just going over what you can do now, that you couldn't do when you first came to see me?

When we had gone over things, this client felt she had got 'enough' from therapy, so was clearly at her 'good enough' point.

Sometimes the good enough point is not established until some way into the therapy, more often than not it is not established until after the miracle/wonderful question. We have a point on the scale where someone was (low point), a preferred future point on the scale, and then we have a good enough point.

A LITTLE BIT ABOUT 'WOBBLY' CLIENTS

What is meant by 'wobbly' clients is that sometimes, just like the therapist, some clients are a bit taken aback that things can change so quickly. In some cases, clients come to therapy not really expecting changes to happen at all, just hoping they will, so things turning around for the better can leave them feeling a bit unprepared, even though they are happy at the changes. It was a client who first told me that they felt 'wobbly' and it is a term that, learnt from a client (our best teachers), I have used many times since. When people are still wobbly about finishing, there are a couple of things we can do that can be helpful.

I offer people a fixed appointment in, say, three months' time with the clear instruction that if, when the time comes, they feel that they do not need the appointment, they just need to ring and let me know, they are not obliged to attend. Or, I offer people an appointment 'in the bank', which they can use within a fixed period of time. So I might say: 'You can contact me anytime in the next three months if you need to see me. If you don't contact me, then I will know you are OK and I will discharge you from the service.' I then put a note in my diary, at an agreed date in the future, something like: 'If Joe not contacted, then discharge'. It is important that the client sees you make the note. I often joke when they leave that meeting that it will be great if I don't see them again.

This last idea also seems to allay the fears of other therapists who are used to working with different approaches or models who do not 'trust' that people can get better in a short period of time or after a few sessions only. I'm not saying that therapists should use this idea just to allay their fears – it is the client we are serving, not ourselves. It is just that those new to a solution focused way of working need to learn to trust the model and trust the client within the model.

RECAP: SUBSEQUENT SESSIONS AND CLOSURES IN SFBT

It is vital to remember that the second and subsequent times a client comes to see the solution focused brief therapist need to be managed by focusing on the initial goals and best hopes and any changes that have happened between sessions. Closing individual sessions and finishing therapy are different. Remember that session closures should leave a client with something to work on outside of the session and should end as a complete session, not leaving things 'hanging' until the next meeting. When we close the therapy or come to discharge a client from our services it should be for clear reasons, mostly client directed and determined.

PERSONAL REFLECTION

Think about your hobbies and interests, about where you would like to be with them. For example, if you like to travel, where are all the places you would love to visit? If you run, how far would you ideally like to be able to run? Then, after the ideal, think about your 'good enough'. What countries would you have to visit to be happy enough? How far would you need to be able to run to be satisfied? Are these things closer than the ideal? If so, they are definitely 'good enough'.

TRY THIS

Think about all the clients you have seen where closures felt 'awkward'. Now, when you see the next new client try to establish in the very first session, along with goals and contracting, how *they* will know, not how *you* will know, when it is time for them to stop coming. Write it in their notes, and when you do close with this client, did it feel better for you as a practitioner?

KEY TERMS USED IN THIS CHAPTER

Closures, subsequent sessions, good enough, client-led.

SUGGESTED FURTHER READING

Many solution focused texts explore subsequent sessions, though few seem to pay heed to endings and closures other than to state that they are related to the initial goals and best hopes. Bill O'Connell probably looks at this more than most in the following book:

O'Connell, B. (1998). *Solution-focused therapy*. London: Sage.

9

WHAT NEXT?

LEARNING OUTCOMES

By the end of this chapter the reader will:

- Appreciate that this skills book is only a start; there is more to read and more to learn
- Appreciate the development of solution focused approaches outside therapy
- Recognize the evidence base for Solution Focused Brief Therapy
- Appreciate the 'additions' that make for a good SF brief therapist

This chapter sets out to show the reader where to go next to develop their solution focused skills or to become a more rounded SF brief therapist. The most important thing for you to remember, however, is to trust yourself, trust the model and, above all, trust the person you are working with.

SUPERVISION

While there are qualified supervisors that are solution focused, and solution focused practitioners who are supervisors, as I write this book there are no formal SF supervision courses or supervision qualifications in many countries. There are differences between being a therapist, receiving supervision and giving supervision, although all will hold to the principle and underpinnings of SFBT.

When attending supervision (as a supervisee), it is important to be clear about what you are taking to supervision and what your best hopes for supervision are. You may want to take cases to outline the work you have done with people, or you may be stuck and want some support in a particular case. Whatever it is, be clear and be prepared. Another good reason for taking notes in a client meeting and writing them up accurately is that you have something concrete to take to supervision.

In essence, you want to be as helpful and useful to your clients as you can and your supervision should aid that process by finding out what has worked, what you have done well and what exceptions there were when things were not going so well with clients. It is good to state and be prepared to accept what is going well. Too often, therapists only bring 'problems' to supervision. In a solution focused supervision session, to do this is not in keeping with the model at all.

In terms of giving supervision, I generally start (unless asked not to) by asking a variant of the question 'What have you done well since we last met?' I also like the BRIEF question (or variant) 'What have you been pleased to notice about your work since we last met?' The assumption, of course, is that I am working with someone who is competent and should be encouraged in that competency. Interestingly, John Wheeler (2010) has created a (self)-certificate of competency based on his supervisory practice that is certainly refreshing. I would recommend it. I will follow up this question with others such as 'What do others notice about your good work?' or client-led interventions such as 'And how would your clients know that you are working well?' I might then ask what the supervisee's best hopes for the meeting are, how they would like to spend the time with me, and how they will know if the meeting has been useful. Just like an SF client session.

Solution focused supervisors need to do two essential things. First, they need to encourage the supervisee to recognize what they are doing well and to do more of it, not focusing over and over on what is not being done well (naturally, the more one does well, the less is not done well). Secondly, supervisors need to use the supervision session as a 'proxy' client session, by asking things such as 'How did you know that was helpful?' or 'What could you have asked/will ask that could be more helpful?' This can be developed even further with questions to highlight the 'listening' skills required by an SF brief therapist. 'What do you think the client got out of your meeting?' 'What did they tell you that let you know you were being helpful?' I might also ask the supervisee to consider asking the client to scale the usefulness of their meeting(s).

It can be especially useful to get the supervisee to think about how their practice is viewed by others too. Kidge Burns (2005: 31) asks the question 'How will you and your colleagues know when you're doing your job especially well, and in which ways is this already happening?'. I particularly like the use of the word 'especially'; it is similar to the use of 'somehow' in client work – descriptive, gentle, encouraging. It is useful, of course, to help the supervisee in their adherence to the SF model by suggesting further reading where appropriate to do so. At the end of the supervision session I will ask if it has been useful and, if so, what has been useful.

Supervision of SF brief therapists should always place the clients' safety and well-being at the top of any agenda. As with any model of therapy, the SF clinical supervisor and supervisee should establish clearly what the respective roles are and who holds responsibility for any casework.

Supervision aims to encourage better practice, provide reflection on current practice and support for the client work being carried out. An SF supervisor, or certainly a supervisor supervising someone in SF practice, needs to be familiar and comfortable with the concept that the therapy is client-driven and collaborative. This is not a top-down, theory-led therapy, nor should supervision be. There is little more disheartening than having one's model misunderstood or, worse still, dismissed in a supervisory relationship.

The supervisor must be open to learning from the supervisee's practice, as the therapist learns from the client. I have often been pleasantly surprised by the insights of both novice SF brief therapists and experienced solution focused practitioners.

This last point is especially poignant given my opening remarks about the lack of formal SF supervision training and qualifications. The SF brief therapist may find that their supervisor knows less about SFBT than they do. The role of the therapist here is to use supervision appropriately, encouraging the supervisor to use SF approaches to supervision. Remember, just because they do not know SFBT inside and out does not mean that they are not extremely skilled in general therapeutic terms or that they have little to offer. I had the same clinical supervisor for 11 years, although she was CBT and psychodynamically trained. Over the years we both learned more about SFBT and she was extremely helpful in asking me: '*So, now putting that issue in an SF framework, what would you do next?*'. The supervisor new to SFBT also has to ensure that they are equipped to supervise in an SF way, so further reading or discussion is advised.

Finally, therapists must ensure that they receive adequate supervision of their practice, as required by their professional association. This differs widely from country to country. For instance, the British Association for Counselling and Psychotherapy (BACP) require a minimum of 1.5 hours of supervision monthly (at the time of writing, in October 2010).

TRAINING

There are numerous providers of training in Solution Focused Brief Therapy/ approaches – I am one of them. Likewise, there are numerous providers who say they offer SF training, which in reality is not. This will happen wherever in the world the reader is. There are established academic courses all over the world, though for many new to SFBT, they will try 'taster' courses of one or two days in duration. This is fine and I would encourage it. Just be clear that what you are paying for, or your employers are paying for, is appropriate. Ask yourself before embarking on any training, what it is you want from the course: an introduction, a refresher, a qualification, continuing professional development (CPD)?

Some time ago the United Kingdom Association for Solution Focused Practice (UKASFP) decided that while they could not 'regulate' training, they could offer some sound advice on what people should be asking before buying in such training. With this in mind, the UKASFP asked me to contribute to the discussion. Before considering training, then, it is worth consulting the UKASFP website and the advice they offer there. I have outlined their guidance below.

Questions to ask if commissioning training

To the trainer(s)

1 Is the trainer insured to deliver training?
2 Can you get a written quote before the training is booked?
3 What are the qualifications and/or experience of the trainer?
4 Can you obtain details of previous training carried out?
5 Does the trainer belong to any professional bodies?
6 Will you see an agenda before the event?
7 Will an evaluation of training be carried out?

For yourself

1 Are you clear about desired outcomes?
2 Do you know what materials/resources the trainer(s) require, such as PowerPoint, IT support, room size, etc.?
3 Are all prospective participants aware of the agenda and outcomes for the training event?
4 Are prospective participants volunteers or is attendance compulsory?
5 Is the course/training stand-alone or is there a plan to implement and follow up?
6 Have you informed the trainer(s) of any special requirements for participants on the course?
7 What happens if you have to cancel the event at short notice? For example, what about fees and charges?
8 Are you clear about charges and payment terms (including travel and other expenses)?
9 Will participants be getting a formal acknowledgement of training (such as a certificate) for use in CPD?

For anyone new to the SF world and reading this book in the UK, I can always recommend that people attend a course at or run by BRIEF. The Brief Therapy Centre is based in London, although it also runs training courses across the UK. The Centre 'started' SF in the UK and are without doubt the biggest training provider in Europe in SF.

BRIEF have their own unique take on SF, which is that they believe in the minimalist approach and spend a lot of time 'honing' SFBT. I did my first SF training with BRIEF, although it was then known as the 'Brief Therapy Practice' (they even 'honed' their name). I am eternally grateful, for they set me on my own SF road, which is not quite so minimalist.

ADVANCED PRACTICE

As I write, I am aware that the Master's course in SFBT in the UK (which I took) is unclear as to its future. There are other courses at diploma and graduate level in the

UK. There are also several courses in the UK at degree level which include SFBT modules. There is also an MSc in 'Solution Focused Thinking and Leadership' in the UK, although this is not 'therapy' *per se*.

There are academic courses in SFBT in Europe, Canada and the USA, and there are many courses, that include modules of SF within wider courses, such as clinical psychology.

If the reader of this text is in the UK, the first port of call for information on SF courses might be the UKASFP. Elsewhere in Europe, contact the EBTA (European Brief Therapy Association), in North America, the SFBTA (Solution Focused Brief Therapy Association), in Australia, the Brief Therapy Institute in Sydney, and in Asia, the Academy of Solution Focused Training. None of this list constitutes an endorsement; it is merely an illustration of the breadth (geographically) of the approach.

REFLECTIVE PRACTICE

All therapists should reflect on their practice, and SF brief therapists are no different. The main way we do this is through clinical supervision. One of the other ways, and a way I thoroughly recommend, is through some of the excellent online discussion groups. Harry Korman's international SFT list throws up complete gems that send me away scratching my chin and reflecting on what I do and how I do it. I 'see' SF practitioners and therapists from all over the world coming online with great questions, great practice examples, and topics as divergent as humour in SF and the role of social construction in SF. It is well worth signing up to: SFT-L@LISTSERV.ICORS.ORG.

In terms of reflective practice, as SF brief therapists we should always adhere to the principle of how what we are doing is being helpful for the people we are seeing. This is our foremost concern. Within this framework, we should be asking ourselves how we can be even more helpful and how we can continually improve our practice.

Reading, of course, is another way to reflect on our practice – not just academic books, but also websites and journal articles. Conferences and workshops are useful for reflective practice too. There are many to choose from, so be selective – which will be of most benefit to the clients I see or, in other words, what can I learn and reflect on?

ACCREDITATION

Accreditation as a therapist means different things in different countries and could take up a book all on its own. It is constantly changing in terms of requirements and legislation, so I propose not to go into too much depth here.

Alasdair Macdonald's *Solution-Focused Therapy* (2007) has a short list of where and how SFBT is officially accredited and recognized worldwide (at that time), and, importantly, looks at some of the ethical issues relating to SFBT (which are often bound in accreditation). I will not, therefore, produce a long list of accrediting bodies here – not least because as soon as I do so it will be out of date.

What I will say is that many of the bodies that accredit therapy and therapists seem to work on processes and assumptions that sometimes make it difficult for SF therapists to meet and/or adhere to. My experience of becoming accredited by the BACP, a leading accrediting organization in the UK, was for the most part positive, though I found myself in a bit of a Procrustean fit where I had to tailor my application and 'evidence' for competency to the association rather than have an acceptance that SFBT was different, even a paradigm shift, from the established, problem focused approaches which are dominant in the therapy world. This is not to say that all accrediting bodies (including BACP) fail to recognize the approach as valid; otherwise, myself and many others would not gain accreditation. There is an issue here, though, that advanced training in SFBT, certainly at an academic level, is not as widely available as other models. My best hope is that there will be more established courses worldwide at Master's level that help define what is required to be a SF brief therapist and that those definitions are accepted by national accrediting bodies.

SF TOOLS

All therapies tend to use tools of one sort or another: assessment tools, functionability (or dysfunctionabilty) tools, outcome measures, and so on. There are some noteworthy SF tools that can be utilized.

The Solution Focused Measure of Occupational Function

This is an excellent tool than can be freely photocopied from *Creating Positive Futures* (Duncan, Ghul & Mousely, 2007). The occupational therapists who devised this tool explain its usage extremely clearly and it can be used in conjunction with other worksheets and tools in the book, as well as partially or wholly as an aid to a therapeutic conversation. I have used parts of this tool on several occasions and found them to be really helpful.

Outcome Rating Scale

This is an easy-to-use outcome measure for effectiveness. It is available free (with conditions) at: http://heartandsoulofchange.com/measures/

Being creative

One of the most exciting things about Solution Focused Brief Therapy is how creative some of its practitioners are, and how creative some of the practice has become. To give some examples...

Yvonne Dolan's 'letter from the future' (2000) is perhaps one of the most used tools in my toolbox of SF creativity. I am not overtly creative myself, but very happy to use creative exercises. I will not describe the exercise in detail, but would encourage you to read Dolan's excellent book. I have adapted this tool so that I ask people something along the lines of: 'If I (or someone else) bumped into you in five years' time and you were able to tell them how things had gone well for you, what would you like to be able to say?'

Here is an example of someone who had been worried that people 'judged' her, that everyone saw her as useless and worthless.

Therapist:	So let's say that you manage to deal with these feelings, like you want to, and in say, four years', five years' time, long after you have finished coming here, I see you in town, what would you like to be able to tell me about your life?
Client:	That I was better.
T:	Better? How? What would be different?
C:	Lots of things.
T:	So we are some years on. Imagine that these years have passed. Lots of things have got better and you are somewhere else in your life, doing something different. What would you like to be able to say … maybe not to me, maybe to a friend that you hadn't seen for a long time?
C:	I'd tell them that I had gone back to college and finished my A levels, and I'd passed.
T:	Which A levels?
C:	Art, English, maybe Psychology, but I wasn't doing that one before.
T:	OK, Art, English and Psychology A levels, that's cool. What else would you like to be able to tell them?
C:	That I didn't pay much attention to the things in my head that told me I was no good, that I knew I was doing OK. They'd know anyway, just from seeing me.
T:	Really, now you've really got me interested. How would they know?
C:	Well, because I was telling them good things, and because I'd be chatty, I'd just be, you know, better, more the real me.

With this particular client, she moved away from telling me what she would like to be able to tell me and moved into what she would like to be telling a friend. This is good.

Strength cards

There are several types of 'strength cards' on the market. I have found them particularly useful with families and young people. They are good for using with people who find it difficult to come up with strengths on their own. Even when people cannot identify strengths themselves using the cards, they are useful in that you can ask clients to identify strengths that others might see in them, or even strengths that they would 'like' to work towards or have.

Hot potato

I have said that I am not that creative, although I will give an example of when I have been creative in a solution focused way, following a client's lead. Mary told me that looking after her disabled husband was so tiring and time-consuming that she was desperate for a break, even an hour, to get out and walk on the hills. I suggested as her between-session task that she did just that. She replied that she could not, even though her husband was encouraging her to take more time out. Her fear was that while she was out she would be so full of guilt for leaving him she would not enjoy the time off.

T: So, even though Bill tells you to get out more, and you know what you would like to do – go for a walk in the hills – guilt is stopping you. That sounds tough, a bit of a dilemma.
C: Guilt is the hot potato that I don't want to hold.
T: I have an idea. I'm thinking on my feet here and it might be a bit bizarre.
C: Go on, I could do with some bizarre.
T: I would like you to go for that walk, Bill wants you to go for the walk, and it is what you want, so seeing as guilt is going to be with you anyway, why don't you warm up a potato, put it in some aluminium foil and take it with you. When it gets too much, throw the potato away. Just an idea, what do you think?
C: I'll give it a go. I must be mad, or you are.
T: Maybe – me that is.

Mary did indeed take the potato, she did throw it away and she told me she laughed out loud when she did. She realized that she did not need to feel guilty, and it was not her last walk.

EXPLAINING SOLUTION FOCUSED BRIEF THERAPY TO OTHERS

First, let me say that there is little need to justify what has become an accepted and well-evidenced model of therapy, although you may need to 'explain' what is still a comparatively new 'therapy' in some places and what has often been practised as simply an intervention, approach or technique that is used outside the therapy world. It is my experience that whenever people are new to something that excites them, be it a new therapeutic approach or a holiday destination, they espouse it loudly and vociferously. Try to hold back, especially in the face of scepticism.

As an SF brief therapist you may come across sceptics – of that there is little doubt. That's OK. My first piece of advice is to try not to convert people – they will resent it, hold on to their own models and generally find you irritating. Don't forget, there are useful skills and interventions in other models too.

My second bit of advice is to just get on with your practice and people will soon see that you are at least having similar outcomes (if not better and quicker ones) as they are, whatever model they employ. If asked by others, feel free to explain and discuss, objectively and factually, but don't be an evangelist.

RESEARCH

This book does not set out to list the SFBT research base in detail; that is ably covered in other texts (e.g. Macdonald, 2007) or on the EBTA website. Indeed, the research base is growing all the time and to list research here means that it will already be out of date by the time this book is published. At the time of writing this (October 2010), Macdonald lists on his website:

> Eighty relevant studies: 2 meta-analyses and 9 randomised controlled trials showing benefit from solution-focused brief therapy, with 6 showing benefit over existing methods. Of 27 comparison studies, 21 favour SFT. Effectiveness data are available from more than 2900 cases with a success rate exceeding 60%.

This impressive evidence base does not include the 40 naturalistic studies that he also details.

FINALLY...

The solution focused journey for most readers is unlikely to have started with this book, though it may have. It is certainly unlikely to finish after reading this book. I know that the solution focused journey that I have been on for the last 16 years has a long way to go. I also know that all the books I read, all the articles I write, all the supervision that I attend will be nothing without two things: an open ear to listen to what clients have to tell me and teach me, and a clear understanding that I cannot know it all, that I will continue to learn and develop in an approach that is still evolving.

I was once asked to present a case study to the team in a psychology department where I was working, showing the 'case flow' and formulation. I panicked for a while and thought that I would be revealed as a charlatan, not a real therapist, as I did not really 'do' those things. I was somewhat stumped, as I believe that each case is different, each 'flow' is different and as SFBT does not espouse a theory, I would not be able to 'show' this case flow and formulation.

I had to balance this with the need to be respectful to my colleagues and to show that I knew what I was doing. So after asking other SF practitioners what they would do, Rayya Ghul, an SF occupational therapist, gave me a good example of a case flow (for which I am indebted). I amended this a little and the result is shown in Figures 9.1 and 9.2.

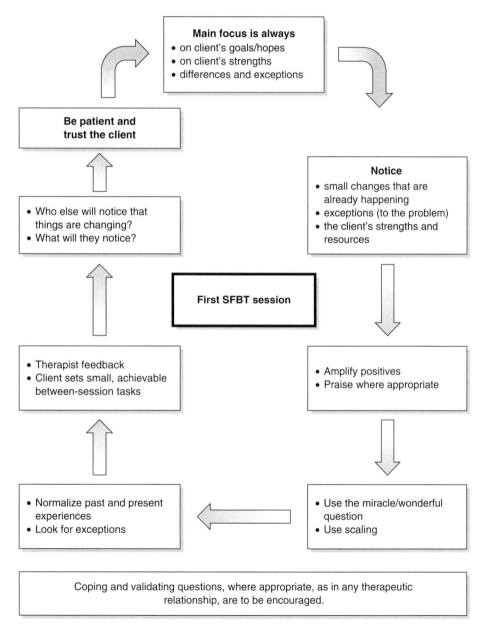

Figure 9.1   Case flow in the first SFBT session

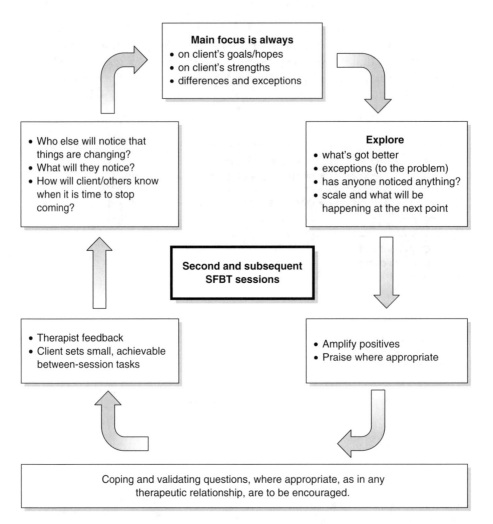

Main focus is always
• on client's goals/hopes
• on client's strengths
• differences and exceptions

• Who else will notice that
  things are changing?
• What will they notice?
• How will client/others know
  when it is time to stop
  coming?

Explore
• what's got better
• exceptions (to the problem)
• has anyone noticed anything?
• scale and what will be
  happening at the next point

**Second and subsequent
SFBT sessions**

• Therapist feedback
• Client sets small, achievable
  between-session tasks

• Amplify positives
• Praise where appropriate

Coping and validating questions, where appropriate, as in any
therapeutic relationship, are to be encouraged.

Figure 9.2   Case flow in the second and subsequent SFBT sessions

RECAP: WHAT NEXT?

This chapter has looked at supervision, research, accreditation and personal
reflection. It has acknowledged that there are topics to be covered outside this
text and that this book will be a starting point for many, as well as a consolida-
tion for some. There has been a brief exploration of some of the training that
exists and some of the tools that can be utilized.

PERSONAL REFLECTION

Ask yourself what are the questions that this book has left you with. Where can you find the answers to those questions? Who can help you with this? What do other SF brief therapists say in their books? Is it different? How and when will you start using some of the interventions and techniques discussed in this book? What SF skills do you already use?

TRY THIS

Sign up to at least one SFBT message list online. Present a case you are struggling with, anonymously, and ask for an SF response to the case. See what you get back – and you will get a lot back, SFBTers are most helpful. Then the next time you meet your client try one thing with the case that is different. That is SF in practice.

KEY TERMS USED IN THIS CHAPTER

Supervision, accreditation, research, creativity, tools, justification, reflection.

SUGGESTED FURTHER READING

Nelson, T. S. (Ed.) (2010). *Doing something different: solution-focused brief therapy practice*. New York: Routledge.
Having just read this book and seeing many references for established authors and classic SFBT texts, try this book for some light, but nonetheless, invaluable reading. I would recommend this book in its entirety, but particularly the following chapters: Chapter 12: Evan George; Chapter 22: Jay Trenhaile; Chapter 25: Vicky Bliss; Chapter 48: Bruce Gorden; Chapter 66: Frank Thomas; Chapter 73: Chris Iveson.

APPENDIX 1: PHOTOCOPIABLE RESOURCES

These resources are available to download from www.sagepub.co.uk/Hanton

This first resource is something that I devised (and have honed) as a guide/prompt for those relatively new to the SFBT approach.

PC RESOURCE 1: FIRST SFBT MEETING

Solution Focused Brief Therapy
First meeting

Client name:

Date:

Presenting issue(s):

Best hopes for coming here?

Strengths, skills, interests (problem-free talk):

Support, family, friends, etc.:

If this work was successful how would you and the client know?

Exceptions (to the problem):

What has made these exceptions more likely to happen?

Wonderful/miracle question:

Scale point after the 'wonderful' thing has happened:

Scale point today: How come? What gets you there on the scale?

What would be happening that tells you that you have moved up the scale?

What would others notice?

Between–session task(s):

Coping questions:

Other comments:

Usefulness of meeting (scale):

What would make the next meeting even more useful?

PC RESOURCE 2: CURRENT/FUTURE ISLAND

I first came across this many years ago when working with young people in the drug and alcohol field. A guy called Jamie Satterthwaite introduced me to the basic concept, and I have since adapted and honed it.

The object of this intervention is to give people a future focus in a visual way. Often people are trying to 'get away' from the 'problems' without thinking too much about the way the future will look.

So, the picture below is copied, either as it is or on a sheet of flip chart paper. The client fills in the entire current island with words that are significant to portray their current life, such as drinking, anger, family hassle, no money, etc. The client also puts on the current island things that are going OK. At this point nothing is written on the future island.

The therapist suggests that there is a body of water between the current island and the future island and asks the client to say what might be on the future island that would encourage them to move/swim towards it, what they might take with them from the current island, and what they might leave behind. It should be recognized by the therapist and the client that even though the current island has 'problems', it is also familiar, whereas it can seem difficult to swim to the future island if we do not know what is on the other shore to meet us. The temptation is for people to 'stay' on the current island with what they know whereas we want to encourage them to move forward. We could get them to scale the current and future islands.

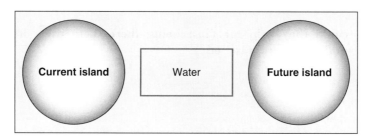

Figure App.1   Current and future islands

PC RESOURCE 3: WHO AND HOW?

This is a short exercise for people to use when they are trying to find solutions and it seems very difficult to do so alone. Ask the client to fill out the sheet below and use this to explore further.

Who and how?

Please answer the questions below. The therapist/worker will then discuss your answers with you.

Q1. Who is important in my life?

Q2. If I were to ask any of the above people to help me to get to where I want to be with my current issue, who would I ask?

Q3. How could they help me (just being there, help me with specific tasks, notice my progress, etc.)?

Q4. Who is the first person I am going to ask to help me? What am I going to ask them to do that is helpful?

APPENDIX 2: USEFUL BOOKLIST AND WEBSITES

BOOKLIST

There are literally thousands of papers and books on SF therapy/approaches now, and I would not suggest that you try to read them all. Several books and papers are referenced throughout the previous chapters. Some are weighty academic tomes and some, like this book, are very specifically geared towards an area of interest. Choose wisely or you will never lift your head from paper. My personal favourites are:

Berg, I. K., & Miller, S. D. (1992). *Working with the problem drinker: a solution focused approach.* New York: W. W. Norton.
This book has been invaluable in my work with drug and alcohol users and was (and is) influential in illustrating the emerging thoughts of Berg and her colleagues at a time when SFBT was less than a decade old.

George, E., Iveson, C., & Ratner, H. (1999). *Problem to solution* (2nd Edn.). London: BT Press.
BRIEF really helped SF ways of working take off in the UK and this is an excellent introduction to Solution Focused Therapy, and one that I read often when I need to be refreshed.

Lipchik, E. (2002). *Beyond technique in solution-focused therapy.* New York: Guilford Press.
Eve Lipchik was one of the original Milwaukee founders of SFBT, along with Steve de Shazer, Insoo Kim Berg and others. This book is a unique departure from the minimalist approach that SF often takes and looks at theory and emotions. I can't say that I agree with everything in this book, but I admire the alternative approach and the 'freshness' of it.

Nelson, T. S. (Ed.) (2010). *Doing something different: solution-focused brief therapy practice.* New York: Routledge.

This book has already become a firm favourite for two reasons. First, the sheer breadth of examples of practice is truly stunning, and it includes the thoughts of a wide range of SFBT practitioners. Secondly, there are 76 chapters in 300 pages, so it is very much a 'dip in' book. It is not a dry academic text, but rather a book full of amusing anecdotes, thought-provoking moments, and a chance to really see how SFBT is not simply following a script.

O'Connell, B. (1998). *Solution-focused therapy*. London: Sage.
Bill O'Connell has a way of writing that simplifies often complex things. This book is a good read and covers a broad range of areas.

O'Connell, B., & Palmer, S. (Eds.) (2003). *Handbook of solution-focused therapy*. London: Sage.
A UK handbook, with chapters from many of the 'leading lights' in their respective SF fields, it covers group work, research, social work, and much more. This book contains easy-to-read chapters following similar formats.

Zeig, J. K., & Munion, W. M. (1999). *Milton H. Erickson*. London: Sage.
Although not strictly a solution focused book, it gives a great overview of the man who, in my opinion, did so much to influence the formation of solution focused ways of working, and the thinking of Steve de Shazer. It is a cracking read.

WEBSITES

Most of the people reading this book will probably have access to the internet. There are thousands of sites and articles dedicated to SFBT, but here are a few that you might find useful. Many of the websites listed here are just a starting point, with links to other sites.

www.solutionfocused.org.uk/
My website, which, of course, I will list. I have useful links to other SFBT websites, and I often change the downloads on the site for others to use.

www.ukasfp.co.uk/
The website of the United Kingdom Association for Solution Focused Practice (UKASFP). Not purely therapy, but a website reflecting the full breadth of SF practitioners in the UK, from social workers, to teachers, to business coaches.

www.solution-news.co.uk/
The website of the free journal of UKASFP. This journal is read worldwide and the website holds current and past copies. It is also a portal for the *Solution Focused Research Review (SFRR)*, a peer-reviewed journal of SF research.

www.brief.org.uk/
BRIEF almost need no introduction. This is their website. While it lists courses and conferences, it also has plenty of useful SF information and tips.

www.ebta.nu/

The European Brief Therapy Association website. It has great pages on current and past SFBT research, and much more besides.

www.sfbta.org/

The website of the North American Solution Focused Brief Therapy Association (NASFBTA). It is a great place to start if you are new to SFBT in the USA or Canada.

www.gingerich.net/

Professor Gingerich has pages on his website dedicated to SFBT research and he helpfully categorizes them as strong, moderate or weak controlled studies. He is also very affable and happy to send any further information when contacted.

www.solutionsdoc.co.uk/

Dr Alasdair Macdonald is a complete powerhouse of knowledge of SFBT and if you ever want to know anything about any research undertaken in SF, he is your man and this is the website to consult. Alasdair has been involved with the EBTA and the UKASFP since their inceptions.

www.sikt.nu/engindex.html

This is the website of Harry Korman and Jocelyne Lopez-Korman. Harry is the founder of the International SFBT message list. He has written many useful articles and has contributed to numerous publications, some of which are available on his website.

REFERENCES

Bachelor, A., & Howarth, A. (1999). The therapeutic relationship. In M. A. Hubble, B. L. Duncan, & S. D. Miller (Eds.), *The Heart and Soul of Change*. Washington, DC: American Psychological Association.

Berg, I. K., & Miller, S. D. (1992). *Working with the problem drinker: a solution-focused approach*. New York: W. W. Norton.

Burns, K. (2005). *Focus on solutions: a health professional's guide*. London: Whurr.

Corsini, R. J., Wedding, D., & Dumont, F. (Eds.) (2008). *Current psychotherapies* (8th Edn.). Belmont, CA: Brooks–Cole.

De Jong, P., & Berg, I. K. (1998). *Interviewing for solutions*. Pacific Grove, CA: Brooks–Cole.

De Jong, P., & Berg, I. K. (2002). *Interviewing for solutions* (2nd Edn.). Belmont, CA: Brooks–Cole.

de Shazer, S. (1985). *Keys to solution in brief therapy*. New York: W. W. Norton.

de Shazer, S. (1994). *Words were originally magic*. New York: W. W. Norton.

de Shazer, S., Berg, I. K., Lipchik, E., Nunally, E., Molnar, A., Gingerich, W. C., & Weiner-Davies, M. (1986). Brief therapy: focused solution development. *Family Process*, 25: 207–21.

de Shazer, S., Dolan, Y., with Korman, H., Trepper, T., McCollum, E., & Berg, I. K. (2007). *More than miracles: the state of the art of solution-focused brief therapy*. London: The Haworth Press.

Dolan, Y. (2000). *Beyond survival: living well is the best revenge*. London: BT Press.

Duncan, L., Ghul, R., & Mousely, S. (2007). *Creating positive futures: solution focused recovery from mental distress*. London: BT Press.

George, E., Iveson, C., & Ratner, H. (1999). *Problem to solution* (2nd Edn.). London: BT Press.

Hanton, P. (2003). Solution-focused therapy and substance misuse. In B. O'Connell, & S. Palmer (Eds.), *Handbook of solution-focused therapy*. London: Sage.

Hayley, J. (1973). *Uncommon therapy*. New York: W. W. Norton.

Hubble, M. A., Duncan, B. L., & Miller, S. D. (Eds.) (1999). *The Heart and Soul of Change*. Washington, DC: American Psychological Association.

Koss, M. P., & Shiang, J. (1994). Research on brief psychotherapy. In A. E. Bergin, & S. L. Garfield (Eds.), *Handbook of psychotherapy and behaviour change*. New York: Sage.

Lambert, M. J. (1992). Psychotherapy outcome research: implications for integrative and eclectic therapists. In J. C. Norcross, & M. R. Goldfried (Eds.), *Handbook of psychotherapy integration* (pp. 94–129). New York: Basic Books.

Lipchik, E. (2002). *Beyond technique in solution-focused therapy*. New York: The Guilford Press.

Macdonald, A. (2007). *Solution-focused therapy: theory, research and practice*. London: Sage.

Mair, K. (1992). The myth of therapist expertise. In W. Dryden, & C. Feltham (Eds.), *Psychotherapy and its discontents*. Buckingham: Open University Press.

McLeod, J. (1998). *An introduction to counselling*. Buckingham: Open University Press.

Miller, G. (2008). The man behind the mirror behind the mirror at BTFC. (An interview by Dr Mark McKergow.) *InterAction: the Journal of Solution Focus in Organisations*, 1(1): 78–88.

Nelson, T. S. (Ed.) (2010). *Doing something different: solution-focused brief therapy practice*. New York: Routledge.

O'Connell, B. (1998). *Solution-focused therapy*. London: Sage.

O'Connell, B. (2007). Solution-focused therapy. In W. Dryden (Ed.), *Dryden's handbook of individual therapy* (5th Edn.). London: Sage.

O'Connell, B., & Palmer, S. (Eds.) (2003). *Handbook of solution-focused therapy*. London: Sage.

O'Hanlon, W. H., & Weiner-Davis, M. (1989). *In search of solutions: a new direction in psychotherapy*. New York: W. W. Norton.

Prochaska, J. O., & DiClemente, C. C. (1983). Stages and processes of self-change of smoking: toward an integrative model of change. *Journal of Consulting and Clinical Psychology*, 51(3): 390–5.

Prochaska, J. O., & DiClemente, C. C. (1986). The transtheoretical approach. In J. C. Norcross (Ed.), *Handbook of Eclectic Psychotherapy*. New York: Brunner/Mazel.

Wheeler, J. (2010). Certificate of competence. In T. S. Nelson (Ed.), *Doing something different: solution-focused brief therapy practice* (Chapter 54). New York: Routledge.

Wills, F. (2008). *Skills in cognitive behaviour counselling and psychotherapy*. London: Sage.

Zeig, J. K., & Munion, W. M. (1999). *Milton H. Erickson*. London: Sage.

INDEX

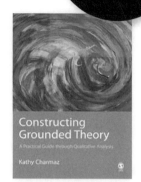

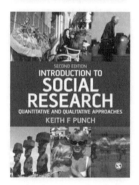
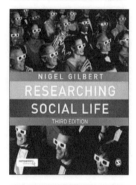
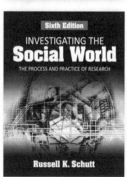

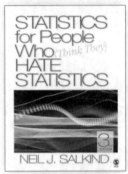

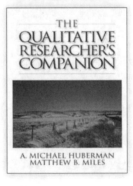